"ANY PARENT ENDURING THE MISERY OF SLEEPLESS NIGHTS WITH BABIES OR TODDLERS WILL FIND THE BOOK BOTH COMFORTING AND HELPFUL."

—*Sunday Times* (London)

Of all child care problems, difficulty with sleep heads the list. Jane Asher and her husband tackled the sleep problems—and won. Now, in a book full of warmth and wisdom, she shares her experience with you, and offers practical, effective advice for helping you transform wakeful midnight hours into . . .

SILENT NIGHTS
FOR YOU AND YOUR BABY

"Pleasurable reading. Even those who never experience such nighttime disturbances will enjoy her funny anecdotes."

—*Nursery World*

"How refreshing! . . . Jane Asher is an original and creative thinker in a field hitherto dominated by some tedious and bombastic child psychology experts."

—*9 to 5* Magazine

WRITTEN AND ILLUSTRATED BY

JANE ASHER

SILENT NIGHTS

FOR YOU AND YOUR BABY

A DELL TRADE PAPERBACK

Published by
Dell Publishing Co., Inc.
1 Dag Hammarskjold Plaza
New York, New York 10017

This work was first published in Great Britain by
Pelham Books Ltd.

Dell ® TM 681510, Dell Publishing Co., Inc.

ISBN: 0-440-58141-9

Printed in the United States of America

First U.S.A. Printing

May 1987

10 9 8 7 6 5 4 3 2 1

MV

Dedicated to the memory of my father,
whose clear, concise, and amusing writing
sets an example I shall always strive to follow.

CONTENTS

Acknowledgments   vii
Foreword by Dr. Penny Stanway   ix
Introduction   11
Feeding   16
The Day Before   25
Environment   33
Getting to Sleep   49
Discomfort   71
Older Babies and Toddlers   82
How to Cope   102
Useful Addresses   109

ACKNOWLEDGMENTS

I would particularly like to thank Dr. Miriam Stoppard, Sheila Kitzinger, and Drs. Andrew and Penny Stanway for talking to me about the book and for their encouragement, support, and advice. I am especially grateful to Penny Stanway for reading through the manuscript and giving me her comments and for writing the foreword.

Many thanks also to my health visitor, Mary Pucknell, to Flora Casement for her help with research, and to the many friends and relations who gave me the benefit of their experience.

Without the encouragement and help of my husband I would certainly never have tackled the drawings, and I would like to express my gratitude to him not only for his love and support but also for providing me with the three beautiful inspirations for the book, Katy, Alexander, and Rory, that make all the sleepless nights worthwhile.

FOREWORD
By Dr. PENNY STANWAY

'There is a time for everything,
and a season for every activity under heaven.'
(Ecclesiastes 3 v.1 **NIV**)

For many parents of young children the time for broken nights seems too long, and it's scarcely surprising that of all child care problems difficulty with sleep heads the list.

Jane Asher writes from experience and with intelligence and wit as she explores how to cope with sleeplessness and broken sleep. She reminds us that if nothing works, a good laugh can put everything into perspective and make the situation bearable. The amusing pictures she paints of her own nighttime antics will be enough to lighten the mood of many a tired parent.

What makes this book special is its acknowledgment that young children often sleep far better with their mothers: a hard fact to swallow for a society which separates children and parents so much. However, the wishes and needs of the rest of the family are not forgotten, and the many practical suggestions will surely help all who find this time hard.

INTRODUCTION

1:00 A.M. Rory (four months) wakes for a feeding. Stagger across the room to his carry cot, blearily lift him out and try to get him latched on before he makes enough noise to wake Alexander (two) next door. Finish feeding and settle Rory back to sleep by about 1:20.

1:40. Just beginning to drift back to sleep when Katy (ten) walks in feeling very hot and miserable. Obviously she's developing the flu, which everyone at school seems to have. Gerald (over twenty-one) gets her some chewable aspirin and after lots of cuddles she falls asleep in our bed, still steaming hot.

2:30. Rory wakes for another feeding—unusual but not unheard of—my good humor beginning to fray a little. Get him back down by three. Can't get back to sleep. Try to remember the dream I was halfway through when first awakened. Eventually begin to doze.

3:20. Alexander shouts from next door. Normally might leave him awhile to see if he might go back to sleep but tonight don't want to risk waking either of other two, so Gerry goes to him. He's wide awake, standing up in the cot, beaming. Much against usual rules we bring him into our bed too, hoping he might settle back to sleep. Bound to catch Katy's flu, but probably already has it. Silence.

4:00. "Daddy, you're a cake." Alexander's wit is rather hard to take at this hour in the morning. G. and I keep eyes tight shut and pretend to be asleep.

"And Mummy's a sandwich.
MUMMY, YOU'RE A SANDWICH."

"Mummy's a very tired sandwich, Alexander."

"No you're not."

"Yes I am. And Daddy is a very tired cake. Look. The cake's asleep. The cake and the sandwich are going to get some more sleep, or they won't be able to play games in the morning." Pause.

4:10. "I'm a tractor and I'm going to crash you. I'M GOING TO CRASH YOU. AND I WANT MY CORNFLAKES."

Katy stirs and Rory starts whimpering for another

feeding, so we decide to abandon the rest of the night and take Alexander downstairs for a predawn breakfast.

As can be seen from this brief outline of a recent, thankfully fairly unusual night in our house, there can be no guarantee of peaceful nights with children of any age. Some people really do seem to produce those amazing babies who do everything by the book, slipping into convenient four-hour feeding schedules and sleeping peacefully in between, but the three we have produced have all, to varying degrees, given us broken nights and worn patches in the carpet from nightly pacing.

It's strange that one of the first questions people ask about a new baby is, "Is he good?"—meaning, of course, "Does he sleep most of the time?" The idea that a little baby can be "good" or "bad" is a very odd one in any case, and so many of the "problems" of children and young babies are more a result of the way our society expects them to behave than of any inbuilt "naughtiness." In a more natural society our babies would be constantly at our sides, waking frequently in the night to feed and never expected to sleep alone in a dark, silent room for hours at a stretch. However, given the way we have organized our lives, we obviously have to gently encourage our babies to sleep through the night. There are many ways of doing this that are worth trying from an early age, before any serious "problems" set in.

Most of this book is concerned with newborn and very young babies, and will I hope be useful in a preventive way, but I have included a section on older babies and toddlers with some hints on the sort of retraining that may be necessary if you are having trouble at night. Unless you are an extraordinarily calm and patient person, a wakeful toddler can be a very disruptive influence in the household. I recently read an article on children who wake in the night, which included the sentence "You may even feel a sort of anger well up

13

inside you as you are called yet again into his room."
May! SORT OF!! Obviously, whoever wrote that has never
experienced a wakeful child at three A.M.!

There is considerable recent evidence to show that a
difficult birth or even certain factors during pregnancy
can affect the way a baby sleeps later on, and if your
baby has difficulties at night it is much less likely to be
due to your handling of him than was previously thought.
People whose babies sleep easily and lengthily don't
understand this and can be very unsympathetic.

I have referred to the baby as "he" throughout the
book because our two last children have been male, so I
tend to think of them when writing about babies in
general, and it is less clumsy than continually referring
to "he or she."

Nowadays, both parents are usually eager to share in
every aspect of baby care. Apart from breast-feeding and
the limitation of time at home due to one or both having
to be out at work, there is of course no reason why both
mother and father shouldn't take on any of the duties
involved in looking after young babies. This book is
addressed to either or both parents, or to any other
person bringing up a baby.

Our third baby, Rory, is so far proving to be the best
sleeper of the three—perhaps partly due to some hard-
learned lessons with the other two—and I hope this
gathering together of our experiences plus ideas picked
up from friends, research, and other parents will be
useful and reassuring to anyone caring for a young baby.
I am lucky enough to have help with Rory during the
day, which has given me the time to write this book
between the demands of the rest of the family and small
excursions into my other work.

I do sometimes wonder if my husband and I are too
soft on the children: one of Alexander's favorite games
at the moment is for me to pretend to be a little boy who

14

keeps calling for his mommy at night. He is the mommy, and when I call he marches straight up to me and says, "I'm going to hit you on the head with a hammer." Perhaps he should have written the book. . . .

FEEDING

BREAST OR BOTTLE?

It has always seemed to me unfair that on the whole, bottle-fed babies sleep longer between feedings than breast-fed ones, and that they tend to sleep through the night at an earlier age. There can be no question that if you want to give your baby the best possible start you will breast-feed him for as long and as fully as possible; it would be far more just if nature would reward you with the sleep you long for during the first few exhausting weeks. Not that bottle-fed babies are all good sleepers—far from it—but cow's milk certainly takes longer to digest and so generally keeps them feeling full longer. Another advantage of bottle-feeding is that it means both parents can share the night feedings equally, but even if the baby is breast-fed, the father can help get him back to sleep or change the diapers. Many fathers nowadays want to join in on as much of the baby care as possible, and the more these difficult early nights are shared the closer will be the bond between all members of the family.

16

Whether with breast or bottle, the first few weeks must be devoted to feeding whenever the baby wants it, which in my case with all three children seemed to be almost constantly, particularly in the evenings.

I felt more and more like a dried prune and the babies looked like the Michelin Man, but I have always felt instinctively, and there is increasing evidence to support it, that you cannot overfeed a baby if you are breast-feeding. Alexander put on weight very quickly in the first few weeks—and as a nine-pounder he had hardly been a bantamweight to start with—and when I took him to be weighed at the clinic I used to get a few raised eyebrows. Luckily there was one woman doctor there who backed me all the way: she had worked extensively abroad and told me that the Samoan women used to carry their babies at the breast and let them feed whenever they wanted, which was almost constantly. This produced big balloons of babies, but they all grew up into beautiful tall slim adults. I can't pretend Alexander is exactly slim at two years three months, but he's getting nicely into proportion now. When I look back at some early pictures of Katy I am amazed how pudgy she was, too, at eight months or so—now she is a very slim, not to say skinny, ten-year-old. Bottle-feeders may have to be a little more careful: it can be harder to lose the weight put on by cow's milk.

It is very important in these early days to snatch sleep whenever and wherever you can, for unless you happen to have one of the very unusual babies who settle quickly into a four- or five-hour pattern, the nights will be very broken indeed. At this stage the only attitude to have is to GO WITH IT—DON'T FIGHT IT. Accept that sleep will be achieved in short bursts rather than the long stretches you are used to, and it will be far less frustrating and worrying.

Even when he is very young there are ways of helping the baby to start to differentiate between day and night, and the way you feed him should be geared to this. Whether he sleeps in your bed or his own crib (see Environment) make sure that the night feedings can be given as quickly and quietly as possible, preferably without turning a light on or making a lot of noise. If breast-feeding, wear a nightgown or pajamas that open easily at the front. Fumbling with difficult buttons while holding a starving impatient baby can be very frustrating, and it's much better and more relaxing for everybody that he should be able to get to the milk as soon as he wakes without having to cry. For bottle-feeders, make sure that everything is on hand and that enough feedings are prepared to see you through the night.

Unfortunately, not all babies will feed thoroughly and quickly until full and then settle peacefully into sleep; often the baby seems to have had plenty but will wake for a little "top up" a few minutes later. If only babies had a sort of milk gauge to show how full they were one would know whether to slip back into a deep sleep or hover around waiting for the final fill-up. Equally, some babies will need burping during and after a feeding, while some will settle down quite happily without. Only experience with your own baby will tell you which sort he is. (See Discomfort.)

There is no need for a young baby to have anything at all other than milk, as this will give him everything he needs, including enough water to quench his thirst. However, if you think you may ever want your breast-fed baby to take a bottle it's a good idea to introduce him to one early on. I was adamant about my second baby's having nothing but breast milk, and from birth onwards, would not allow him to have any water, glucose, etc. I

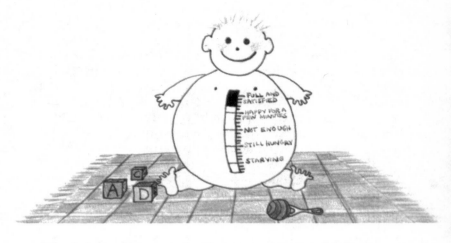

"If only babies had a sort of milk gauge to show how full they were."

did regret it, since later on, when I wanted to express milk and leave it for him during the occasional evening out or as a break from night feeding, he would have nothing to do with a bottle. With my third baby I have been far more flexible and find that the occasional drink of water, fennel, or diluted fruit juice can be very useful between feedings and for getting him used to taking a bottle. I am, however, very much against complementary bottles of milk under six months, as even one can undo much of the good that you are doing by breast-feeding, and need hardly ever be necessary if you breast-feed often enough to maintain a good supply. Early introduction of cow's milk or soy milk can set up allergies for life, and the results of these could prove far more disruptive to good sleep later on than keeping up the night feedings in the early stages! Tempting as it may be to leave a bottle of formula for someone else to give at night so you can have a little well-earned rest, this should be avoided for the first three or four months at least. Instead, try expressing.

Expressing can seem almost impossible at first, but with perseverance and practice it does get easier: the secret is to take it very gently and calmly and not expect too much of yourself. When I first started trying after having Katy I couldn't believe I would ever produce any measurable amount; after perhaps ten minutes of very uncomfortable squeezing and manipulating I might find a few little drops in the bottom of the container. I couldn't bear to transfer it into a bottle, since even the tiny residue left behind represented so much time and effort and there was nowhere near enough to feed her anyway. I soon gave up.

After I had Alexander I tried again with the rubber-bulb-and-glass type of expressor but found it very uncomfortable, and since he wouldn't take a bottle anyway I didn't persevere. Now, however, since having Rory, I am quite proficient. I started by using the type of gadget that looks like a giant syringe: I found it much more comfortable and successful than the bulb one, and the only problem was how to use it in any sort of privacy. For some reason Katy and Alexander found it hilariously funny and would get fits of giggles as they watched me struggling away.

If you get really enthusiastic and want to leave large amounts on a regular basis, it may be worth renting an electric pump from your local branch of La Leche League. It's expensive, but it can be worthwhile if you need to fit in a few hours of work each week, or have a busy social life. I have rented one while I am feeding Rory: it does make you feel rather like a cow in a dairy but it's wonderfully easy to use and you can produce plenty of milk very comfortably. The privacy is no easier— Alexander is so fascinated by any type of machine or motor at the moment, he spotted the pump the minute I brought it in the house, and trying to relax and allow my let-down reflex to work while my every move is watched from close proximity by an eagle-eyed two-year-old mechanic is not easy. He even announced in the middle of a rather quiet lunch with some friends the other day, "I want to see your breast pump." Quite a conversation stopper.

Keep everything scrupulously clean and sterilized, and put the milk straight into the refrigerator, where it can be kept for three days, or, when cooled, can be frozen and kept for three months. Never mix together small quantities of different temperatures—make sure they have been cooled in the refrigerator before adding one to another. My health visitor had a brilliant idea for storing it: use the Playtex plastic bottle liners, which are presterilized and can be slipped straight into a bottle. You don't have to use the complete Playtex system; they work perfectly well in an ordinary bottle with the top screwed down over the plastic.

When you have accumulated enough feedings in the freezer, you can ask your husband, mother, or a friend to do a night for you, and even just one whole night's sleep can be an enormous boost. If you are bottle-feeding ideally your partner will be taking his turn nights in any case. Sometimes the father can feel very shut out in the early days by the closeness of mother and baby, and the more he can share in the everyday (and night!) feeding and changing, the more quickly his relationship with the child will grow.

GETTING BIGGER

After a few weeks, if your demand-fed baby is still demanding his feedings rather more often than you may like, it is worth gently starting to persuade him to go for longer periods between them. This is where his being used to a bottle pays off. When he seems hungry but has had a recent feeding, try offering him some water, very diluted fruit juice, or an herb drink. It's much better if this can be given by Dad—the smell of milk on the mother may well start the baby clamoring for a breast-feeding when he could do quite well without. This applies to day or night: if he learns to do without milk for longer stretches during the day his stomach will gradually adjust, and of course if some of the night feedings are replaced by water or juice he may well stop bothering to wake up for them. Never let him be unhappy or hungry—this can only work against you and make everybody miserable. If he really still needs frequent feedings he must have them. When Rory had a cold recently he went back to feeding every hour right through the night for four or five nights. Just as I was beginning to despair, he suddenly returned to his relatively reasonable once every two to three hours.

SOLIDS

At about four months, or when your doctor advises, you will start him on solids. This may or may not help the sleep pattern but, tempting as it may be, the prospect of a better night's sleep is no justification for cramming the baby with as many calories as he can take. The instinctive feeling that a large, late night supper will help see him through the night is probably a false one; good satisfied sleep seems to depend more on the quantity of food taken during the day as a whole (although even with a baby just starting on solids sometimes a teaspoon of something tasty and filling at about six o'clock can make quite a difference that night).

"The instinctive feeling that a large, late night supper will help to see him through the night is probably a false one"

23

ALLERGIES

There is much interest in this subject at the moment, and I'm sure there is a great deal yet to be discovered about the way food affects us. Certainly many parents of so-called "hyperactive" children claim remarkable improvements in them if they are put on diets free from preservatives, colorings, and artificial flavorings. This sounds very reasonable: I think we may look back in amazement in a few years at the large amounts of pesticides, chemicals, and so on that we all eat. If you believe your child may be truly hyperactive, do have him examined by a pediatrician.

The most commonly quoted suspect in the additive list is the orange coloring tartrazine, or Yellow No. 5, as it is usually called on a list of ingredients. This is present in most types of orange soda, among other things, which children tend to drink in great quantities. Even if your child is not hyperactive, if he tends to wake at night or gets fractious very easily there's no harm in cutting out this additive to see if there's any improvement. I have removed it from our family's diet just to be on the safe side.

Sugar has also been blamed for behavior disturbances, and as this is so very bad for children's teeth it can only be a good thing to cut it out as much as possible. We have always had a Saturdays Only rule for sweets in our house, and we try to save cakes and cookies for parties and special occasions.

Many other foods have been found to cause allergic reactions in certain babies and children, and recently published reports have urged doctors to take the whole subject more seriously and pressed for further research. If you feel your child might be reacting to a food it may be worth writing down everything he eats until you narrow the field to a few suspects. Do talk to your doctor about your child, and if necessary ask to see an allergy specialist.

It is often suggested that babies may be allergic to cow's milk (see page 19).

THE DAY BEFORE

From a very early age the amount of time that a baby is active and stimulated during the day can affect the amount that he will sleep later. In the first few weeks sleeping and waking is fairly haphazard, but even in these early stages one can help the baby to start differentiating between day and night. Quite apart from tiring him out, it is essential for the baby to be talked to, smiled at, and generally stimulated to ensure the best possible development of his brain and faculties. Right through childhood, intellectual activity can be as tiring as physical exertion—very often the first time a child sleeps really well is after starting school.

FIRST FEW WEEKS

During the day try to keep the baby in a place where he can hear family life going on around him. Put him in a carry cot or basket rather than in his crib, so that you can move him around easily. While he is lying awake, hang a brightly colored mobile within view or position

"The amount of time that a baby is active during the day can affect the amount he will sleep later"

26

him so that he can see out the window. If you are lucky enough to have somewhere out of doors where he can lie in his carriage, put it under the trees, where he can watch the fascinating changing patterns of light and dark.

At night, although he may be awake and asleep in the same proportions as during the day, try to make the wakeful periods as unstimulating and boring as possible. Don't chat to him or turn the light on while changing and feeding.

GETTING BIGGER

As he begins to take in more of the world around him it becomes easier to make the difference between day and night more marked. There are some excellent pieces of equipment that can be indispensable in making his day as enjoyable and active as possible.

When he is about a month old, it is worth investing in a bouncing cradle. The great advantage of one of these is that he can watch you and the rest of the family from a comfortable, propped-up position and can kick his legs and wave his arms freely, which will make the canvas chair gently bounce. It is better than propping him up on cushions, where, however carefully you do it, he will almost certainly have sunk into an undignified and uncomfortable heap a few minutes later. It's surprising how much movement can be achieved by persistent squirming and kicking. You can buy brightly colored beads or jolly little men that fix onto the bouncing cradle and very soon he will try to reach forward and touch them. I found with Alexander that it made it more interesting for him if I varied the beads by covering one of them with shiny silver foil or different-colored paper—it was fascinating to see him try to touch the "new" one. If you do this, make sure the paper is securely fastened so there's no danger of the baby managing to get it off and put it in his mouth. Move the chair from time to time so that he can either see you or some other interesting view—the television can be the most wonderful source of light, color, and sound to stimulate a baby. It somehow makes me feel rather guilty to be switching on the television for a three-month-old baby, and I'm irrationally quite pleased when there's something on that could be termed educational. If television had been marketed as a "baby-stimulator" I'm sure I wouldn't feel that way: there really couldn't be anything better for the purpose. As soon as he is able to grasp things, give him a noisy, colorful rattle to wave about.

Of course, not all babies will settle happily into sitting in a chair or lying awake in a cradle; there are some who seem to be content only while being carried around. For these I am sure it is right to give them what they want. Buy a sling or baby carrier, and accept the fact that the housework or whatever will have to be done with your baby attached. In many other cultures this is the general rule, and it certainly gives the baby a wonderful sense of security and comfort. If his father or an older brother or sister can take a turn to give you a break, so much the better—it is surely preferable to hearing an unhappy baby crying in his crib. The only snag is that carrying him around will be very likely to make him drop off to sleep (see page 57), so he may not have as much time active and awake during the day as you would wish. Try some loud conversation as you move around, and every few days have another try at putting him into a baby bouncer. The clinging phases often come and go, particularly if he is indulged in his need to be carried when necessary and not left to cry.

WATER

Playing in water is not only enormous fun but very tiring for babies and toddlers. Sometimes bathing the baby in the evening can help his sleep and can become part of a winding-down ritual, which will be very important as he grows older. If Dad is out at work all day this can be a very good time for him to take over the care of the baby and for them to enjoy each other's company. Start to introduce bath toys into the routine, and make the whole procedure fun and exhausting.

As soon as possible, take him swimming—there are now a number of swimming pools around the country

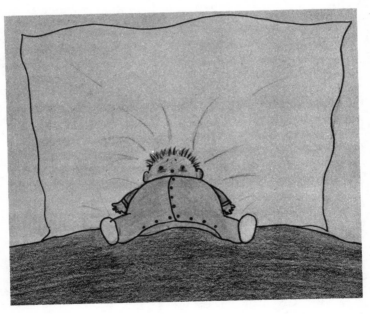

"However carefully you prop him up on cushions he will almost certainly sink into an undignified and uncomfortable heap."

which provide especially warm water for babies and toddlers. Don't take him if the water is cold: not only will the baby hate it, but you will get very shivery yourself, having to stand still so much of the time. Both of you will be miserable, and it might put the baby off what should be an extremely enjoyable activity. Many places have classes for mothers and babies, and these are well worth joining—apart from the fun and, with luck, the good sleep that will follow, it is very important that the baby should learn to swim as soon as possible, for safety's sake. If you can take a friend with you the first few times, so much the better. You'll want to get the baby dried and dressed as quickly as possible after swimming, and it can be a bit miserable trying to handle a slippery wet little creature on a shallow wooden bench while shivering in your own soaking swimsuit.

EXERCISE

Usually at about six months—or earlier, if he can support his head with complete confidence—the baby can start using a baby bouncer. This is a sling seat made from material hung on a strong spring, with the baby's feet just touching the floor, so that when he kicks he bounces up and down vigorously. It is suspended either from a frame of its own or from a hook in the ceiling—if you are using one of the Lullaby hammocks (page 41) then one or two strategically placed hooks can be used for both. These bouncers have very good "tiredness value" and are great fun. Katy would be happy in one for about ten minutes—very good going for her—and it's amazing how much you can accomplish in that time if you're the parent of a restless baby. The rarity of having two free hands makes you really appreciate it when you do, and you zoom around getting six things done at once.

"Playing in water is not only enormous fun but very tiring."

Once he starts pulling himself up on things and showing signs of trying to stand, one of the baby walkers on wheels is a very good way of encouraging him and using up energy.

As a general rule, bring out toys, rattles, books, and so on in rotation, rather than always the same selection every day, to produce as much variety as possible and avoid boredom. There are now toy libraries that you can join. It's always the forbidden things like handbags, keys, china ornaments, glasses, and so on that prove irresistible to inquisitive fingers, so try to keep surprising him with similarly exciting new "toys" of his own. Alexander, for instance, had his own set of keys, made up of lots of old unused ones put into an old handbag, which he would play with for hours.

Going out in the fresh air from as young an age as possible nearly always improves a baby's sleeping. Taking the carriage out to do the shopping or for a walk in the park, then later on the stroller, not only makes the baby's day more interesting but will certainly help to tire him out. Some supermarket carts are exactly wide enough to set a bassinet in sideways, and many stores have assistants who will help you to pack up and load the groceries. My babies always seem to get hungry just as I reach the line at the cash register and have to be taken out and carried to prevent an uproar. I have breast-fed in the most extraordinary places, but I think a supermarket checkout line would be going a bit far. I did have to stop on the way back from the village shop on a country walk once and breast-feed by the side of the road: it felt rather like something out of Thomas Hardy.

Try to find a local mother and toddler group and use the local playgrounds.

ENVIRONMENT

WHERE TO SLEEP

One of the first and most important decisions to be made is where the baby is going to sleep. In many other cultures the baby automatically sleeps with its parents, often in the same bed and sometimes until the age of six or seven. This naturally avoids many of the so-called sleep problems that we in the West suffer from: we expect a great deal of a newborn baby when we banish him to a separate, silent room all on his own after he has spent nine months in the warmth and security of his mother's womb. Many Western families are now bringing their children into the same bedroom and even into the family bed, but this may not always be the perfect solution.

In the early stages, if you are breast-feeding, there is no doubt that it is infinitely more restful for both mother and baby to have him next to you in bed. Neither of you has to wake fully when the baby is hungry—you can just roll over and feed him as you doze, and since he will hardly need to cry to alert you there is more chance that the rest of the family will be undisturbed. It's a lovely feeling to have a warm snuggly baby next to you in bed to cuddle. The worry that many people have about lying on top of their babies and suffocating them is a false one; research has shown that unless the parents are drunk or drugged they will be aware of the baby even in deep sleep, and move away from him when necessary. I do think, though, that it is worth pushing the bed against a wall and having the baby between you and the wall, and when you feed the other side, between you and your husband, so that you are confident he will not fall out— otherwise you may spend much of the night tense and half aware of keeping him safe, which means you won't get much relaxed sleep. If you can't put the bed against the wall push a large piece of furniture against it, or two heavy chairs. And if you're a single parent or your husband is away obviously you will have to take these precautions on the other side as well.

There are of course some disadvantages to having the baby in bed with you. Theoretically he should space out his feedings naturally so that after a few months he is only waking once or twice in the night, but I found with Alexander that this didn't really happen. He slept in bed with us from birth, as I found it much more trouble to keep getting in and out of bed to feed him, and also of course there was the enormous advantage that instead of the sometimes impossible business of getting him back to sleep after a feeding by rocking, singing, patting, and so on, he would just drift off peacefully next to me, with no effort on my part at all. For the first few months it worked very well, and I got much more sleep than I had with Katy who had slept in a cradle.

Alexander was a large baby who needed to breast-feed very often, but as he got bigger he did indeed start to sleep longer between sessions. Then, however, he started gradually to return to the frequent feedings, and eventually couldn't sleep at all unless constantly at the breast. This I began to find very tiring, and when I did decide to move him to his own bed it was a long and difficult process.

Film taken over a few nights of a baby sleeping next to its mother has shown that the baby rarely goes for longer than twenty minutes or so between feedings, certainly when newborn. I have no doubt that having the baby next to you is the natural way and that the frequent small feedings are as nature intended, but in our society, where one is expected to keep going for most of the day, a certain amount of uninterrupted sleep at night is obviously essential. As with so many aspects of baby care, the success of sharing the bed depends on the temperaments of both mother and father, as well as that of the baby, and must remain an individual decision. With Rory, I took a midway course, and had him in bed for the first few weeks, then transferred him to a cradle once he was in the habit of going straight back to sleep after feedings. At the time of writing this has so far worked pretty well. He does still wake for night feedings, but at least he goes back to sleep in between, and the gaps are definitely getting longer.

Apart from the possible difficulty of getting the baby out of the family bed and into his own, another problem of bed sharing can be the reaction of other members of the family. Many husbands would be very unhappy at the idea of a third member of the family in the marital bed; if it is going to cause any friction then it is obviously not worth it. If your husband is uncertain but not definitely against it, it may be worth a try—he will probably get more sleep with the baby in the bed being fed the instant he wakes than he would being awakened by screams from a cradle across the room or next door.

There is the common worry that a couple's sex life

will suffer, but in practice this is rarely a problem; a deeply sleeping baby is pretty oblivious to everything going on around him, and in the words of the song "love will find a way"! However, there will undoubtedly be many husbands who will resent the intrusion of the baby into bed, and for these families another arrangement must be made. I'm lucky enough to have a partner who will go along with anything that will help me to get more sleep—I can be so unbearably irritable and short-tempered after a particularly bad night that all the family has learned how important it is that Mother gets some rest.

Another reaction to be taken into account is the jealousy of the siblings. It may be hard enough to take the arrival of a new baby without discovering him in the parents' bed. Some tactful transferring early in the morning may be necessary to avoid discovery. Alternatively, be prepared for an invasion by the other child or children and to eventually all sleeping together in a true "family bed."

If you do decide to have one or all of them in with you, you will need an extra-large bed so that you can all sleep reasonably well. As these are extremely expensive to buy, a better solution is either to construct a simple wooden platform on which you put two mattresses crosswise or to push a couple of beds together, again, placing the mattresses across them. Even if the children don't sleep with you all the time, it is wonderful to have a large comfortable space for them to snuggle into when ill, or even for cozy Sunday mornings all together. The main point to remember is that there is absolutely nothing wrong with bringing children into your bed if it feels natural to you, and that no one should let comments by neighbors or relatives put them off. Some parents have their first good night's sleep for years after bringing the normally sleepless child into their bed. I

"The beautiful cradles you see in the big stores are very tempting."

am sure that many babies and young children are very lonely in rooms on their own, and this may well be a factor in their waking at night.

If you decide not to have baby in the same bed the next decision is where to put him. If you are feeding on demand you will certainly be up several times in the night at first, and it's much easier to have him in the same room. Right next to your bed can be a very good place, since you can reach him quickly and probably without getting out of bed. The only snag is that if you are basically lazy, as I am, you may find that you don't put him back after feeding—it's so easy to snuggle down and drop off together rather than make the effort to tuck him back into his crib or cradle and maybe have to do some rocking, patting, and singing before you can creep back into your own bed. If this happens several times you're back to square one—he's sleeping in your bed. I have had to put the crib over on the other side of the bedroom so that I'm forced to get out of bed each time he wakes—by the time I reach him I'm just about fully awake and strong-minded enough not to take him back into bed. If he's the sort of baby who does need some walking or rocking after a feeding to get back to sleep, this is a way Dad can share in the nights even if you are breast-feeding.

If he's a very noisy sleeper or you have a tiny bedroom, you may not want to share it with him. In this case, an adjoining room is the best. Even if you can hear him via a baby alarm, padding along corridors or up and down stairs in the middle of the night is not much fun, and the sooner you reach him the less worked up he will be and the more likely to have a calm feeding and go off to sleep again. He must be somewhere where you are confident you will hear him without having to strain, or you will never relax enough to go deeply to sleep. If you are a very light sleeper or he is a noisy sleeper, a room next door can even be preferable to being in your room; otherwise you will wake at all his little snuffles and gurgles when he is not really ready for a feeding.

Make the room as light, bright, and cheerful as possible, and put up some interesting pictures and mobiles. Later on, when he begins to understand that it is his own bedroom, it will be very important that you have made it somewhere he enjoys being.

If you are not sure that you will easily hear him, fix up a baby alarm, so that you can sleep without worrying. Some of them have a talk-back switch so that you can comfort the baby by the sound of your voice, but the only time I ever tried to use one Katy nearly leapt out of the crib with the shock. I suppose your mother's voice suddenly booming out from a little box must seem a bit strange.

AND IN WHAT

When you have decided on where he will sleep, you must choose what he is going to sleep in. The beautiful cradles draped in ribbon and lace that you see in the big stores are very tempting, but quite unnecessary and very expensive. As long as he is warm, securely wrapped, and lying on something reasonably soft, a baby can sleep in just about anything. It's best to have something quite small at first; a full-size crib can give him too much overwhelming space, and it can be difficult to make him feel cozy and secure. Since he will probably have been in a hospital crib for a few days, something of a similar size is probably suitable. The old-fashioned idea of using a drawer or box is perhaps a little too practical—it's not every day a new baby comes home and it's enjoyable for everybody to put the baby into something reasonably attractive. A wicker baby basket is not too expensive, is easy to move around, and looks very pretty. Make sure it is lined all round the sides or else buy or make a lining to fit it to prevent drafts. Alternatively, if you are going to be traveling later on with the baby, a carry cot is the answer, since it can be safely strapped onto the back seat of the car and is easy to move around.

The carry cot or basket should be put on a sofa, low table, or two chairs pushed together, since the floor would be too drafty and very uncomfortable for you to reach. If you already have the crib that the baby will be moved into later, the carry cot can be placed inside it.

If you can afford it it is of course ideal to have a proper cradle. It is rather an extravagance, since he will not be in it for more than a few months, but a cradle can look very attractive, and, if you buy a rocking one, can be very helpful in getting the baby to sleep. Up until this century most cradles were made with rockers, and I can't understand why this practice didn't continue—all babies are soothed by movement, and it's much less tiring just to reach out an arm and rock the cradle that to take the baby out and walk around the room or rock him in your arms. There are now one or two rocking cradles available, and it may be worth investing in one right away.

Most cradles, of course, rock or swing from side to side: an up and down movement is even more soothing, more like the motion experienced while inside the mother.

In 1969 a London doctor discovered that babies stop crying if rocked up and down at a critical speed of sixty to seventy times a minute. A recent invention has made it possible to achieve this very simply. Mr. and Mrs. Owens were desperate with their crying baby, until they discovered that she could be calmed by their holding the carry cot between them and lifting it up and down. Howard Owens set about making a net to hold a carry cot suspended by a strong spring from a hook in the ceiling—it worked so well that he started to manu-

facture these "Lullababy hammocks" and sell them by
mail order from his home. I only wish I'd had one for
Katy and Alexander: Rory is relatively so easygoing
that it's hard to tell how effective it is for him, but there
are many satisfied parents to testify to its success. The
Owenses even give a "peace or money back" guarantee.

Vertical rocking is nothing new. In parts of Africa
they suspend their babies in hammocks to achieve a
very similar effect. They now make cradles that stand
on a spring at each corner that will rock up and down at
a push. I should think it would be possible for a handyman to construct a similar one—or a Lullaby hammock
like the Owenses'—at home. A wooden box with a spring
at each corner in which you place the carry cot should
be very effective.

For daytime naps put the carry cot anywhere that is
conveniently within earshot. If the weather is mild and
you are lucky enough to have somewhere available, the
baby could spend some time out of doors. Make sure
that the carry cot or carriage is covered with a net to
prevent any possible danger from cats.

"Little Stone Age babies must have lain on some very interesting furs."

As soon as you feel the baby is finding it uncomfortable in his cradle or carry cot or is trying to sit up, usually at four to six months, then move him to a full-sized crib. A traditional drop-sized one is best—make sure it conforms to the required safety standards, particularly as regards the distance between the bars, which should be no more than about 2⅜ inches (6 centimeters) apart.

BEDDING

Whichever type of cradle you choose, the bedding is very important and can be a factor in encouraging peaceful sleep. Make sure you buy one of the modern mattresses, with ventilation holes at one end so that there is no danger of suffocation. Cover this with an elasticized bottom sheet which will stay smooth and unwrinkled. If you suspect that your baby may be waking because he is cold, you could try one of the thermal pads underneath him—however warm you make the room it is not the same as lying on something which is warm in itself, which of course is how it would be if the baby were lying on his mother. There are special electric pads available such as they use in hospitals, but I find the thought of electricity in a baby's bed rather alarming, especially since there is a possibility of his being wet in the night. You could use one to warm up the crib and then turn it off when you put him to bed, but a hot-water bottle removed at the last minute would do the job just as well.

Alternatively, you can replace the undersheet with one of the lambskins which have become very popular recently. These are claimed to keep the baby warm in winter and cool in summer, and many people swear that the baby sleeps much better and also seems happier lying on one while awake during the day. The theory is that the wool caresses the baby as he moves around. There is no danger of suffocation, since air can circulate freely through the strands of wool. Research has shown that babies do seem to feel very secure and comfortable on one of these, and in premature baby units it was found that babies kept on lambskins actually gained weight faster than those on ordinary sheets. Certainly one great asset is that if the baby does seem very happy on a skin you can lie him on it during the day and take it with you traveling, and he will have a constant source of security. In one hospital they tried making artificial lambskins and they didn't have the same effect—the babies sucked at the man-made fibers and tried to eat them and didn't seem happy at all.

I have tried one for the purposes of the book, and Rory certainly seems very happy on it; he sort of snuggles into it as he settles down, and he drifts off to sleep more easily than he did on a sheet. It's difficult to know if he feels cool in summer and warm in winter; I've tried asking him, but at three months he just won't give me a straight answer. I shall have to write an appendix to the book when he's old enough to tell me.

Again this is nothing new; the use of animals skins for babies has been common practice in many parts of the world, including our own, for hundreds of years. Little Stone Age babies must have lain on some very interesting furs. It is extraordinary how in so many ways we are coming full circle; having been through the modern ideas of bottle-feeding, separate beds, technological childbirth, and so on, our society seems to be gradually reverting to a simpler, more natural way of looking after our babies. Rory looks quite medieval on his lambskin in his wooden rocking cradle. If we can only combine the best of both worlds and use our wonderful modern technology in a gentler, less regimented, more loving way, we should be able to produce some very healthy, happy children.

Whether you have an undersheet or a lambskin, you will of course need to cover the baby with something for much of the year; here again there are many choices. In most cases it's best to have a cotton or polyester sheet between baby and blanket, since wool can be rather itchy and uncomfortable and in a few may even cause an allergic reaction. The sheet can be tucked into the mattress very tightly, thus making the baby feel secure and having an effect like swaddling (page 53), or you can swaddle him properly by wrapping the sheet right around him and he won't need another one over him. You can either buy little crib sheets or cut up some old full-sized ones of your own. Then cover the top sheet with a light but warm woolen blanket or two, depending on the temperature of the room—some of the man-made fiber ones are very good but probably not quite as warm. Finish with a pretty cover if you like, perhaps when the grandparents come to visit.

Alternatively, a baby's quilt can replace sheet and blankets and is very light as well as warm. Although they are not really meant to be tucked in, if you feel the baby likes it, as so many do, you can always turn the quilt sideways and tuck it firmly under the mattress.

Never give a baby a pillow—it is quite unnecessary and can even carry a slight risk of suffocation. You can now buy ones made with ventilation holes like the mattress, which is an improvement, but I still see no point in having one; it may look more comfortable to us because we are so used to sleeping with pillows, but to a baby it is more natural and healthier for the back and shoulders to sleep without one.

Don't overload the baby with bedding—lightness with warmth is the key. Recent research has shown that if anything, we tend to overheat our babies. It's less dangerous to be slightly too cold than to be too hot. When he

44

moves into a full-size bed the alternatives in bedding are very similar. A quilt is probably the simplest and most comfortable choice.

NIGHTWEAR

For dressing the baby himself it's obviously not essential to have pajamas or a nightgown in the early stages, but it is a good idea to change into something different at bedtime, since it all helps to underline the difference between day and night. If not pajamas then a comfort-

"It is a good idea to change into something different at bedtime."

able Babygro sleeper over an undershirt is quite adequate, but if he proves later to be the type to fling off all his bedclothes, you may need to buy one of the warmer all-in-one sleep suits with feet. If you do buy pajamas for an older baby, make sure the top is long enough to tuck well into the trousers or that it has elastic loops and buttons to keep the two halves together—there's nothing more miserable than a cold midriff in the middle of the night. If he is a very active baby you can try to guard against later problems of his climbing out of his crib in the middle of the night by putting him now into a cozy baby bag. If he has always worn one at night he will not object to being in one later on, and it will make climbing almost impossible.

Don't be tempted to overdress him; as with bedding and room temperature we often tend to overheat our babies. In the summer on a very warm night an undershirt and diaper will be enough, or even just a diaper in really hot weather.

If you find it difficult to change his diaper in the middle of the night without waking him up completely, slip a disposable diaper pad inside his usual one. This will absorb considerably more wetness and probably keep him comfortable right through the night; it may look bulky but he almost certainly won't mind. A one-way liner also helps to keep his skin dry and prevent diaper rash. Babies seem to vary considerably as to whether they mind being in a wet diaper or not—if yours does, he must of course be changed as soon as he's uncomfortable. But have everything ready nearby for as many changes as you think he may need, and do them as quickly and quietly as possible without turning the light on. If the diaper is just wet, you may be able to change him with one hand while feeding him; I could sometimes manage it. It feels rather satisfying to be dealing with both ends at once. If you can afford them, disposable diapers are wonderfully quick and easy, and the new elastic-legged ones are far more leakproof than they used to be: it also means no depressing bucket of soaking diapers for you to deal with in the morning. In cool climates he will nearly always need an undershirt. I have always used "onesies," the type that snap between the legs. They seem more cozy than the short type, help keep the diaper in position, and prevent riding up, which makes a cold gap in the middle of the night.

LIGHT AND DARK

The amount of light in the room will not affect a new-born baby one way or the other, but it is a good idea to have it fairly dark to help him recognize nighttime. Don't have it pitch black; that would make it difficult to feed and change him without having to turn on a light. A door slightly ajar with a light left on outside is preferable to buying a special night-light, which he may get so used to that it will be difficult for him to sleep without it later on. You can buy a low-watt bulb to make it less expensive. There seems to be an instinctive fear of complete darkness that appears in many young children, whether they have been brought up with or without a light, and I am against trying to make them "brave it out." This may appear to work, but it may be that they are only bottling up their fear to please you, and it may manifest itself in some other way. It seems to me unnecessarily cruel.

TEMPERATURE

The room need not be excessively warm. Many hospital nurseries are kept at a high temperature because some of the smaller babies may tend to be cold, but there is no need to keep the baby's room at the same level once you get home. Don't judge it entirely by the way you feel, however, since babies spend much of their time immobile and so will generate less heat than you do. Just make sure the room is comfortably warm and that the air doesn't feel cold to breathe, especially for a newborn baby or one that is unwell. It may be cheaper to buy a separate heater for the baby's room rather than to step up the heating for the whole house. If you've ever worried as to whether the baby is too hot or cold, gently feel the back of his neck: it should feel nicely warm. Cold hands or feet are not necessarily an indication that he is too cold altogether.

NOISE

As with light and dark, a newborn baby's sleep will be relatively unaffected by noise. Many people recommend that he should sleep surrounded by a certain amount of sound so that he will become used to it and be able to sleep more easily later on, without having to have complete silence. I'm not sure this really works—my sister and I were brought up identically, yet she always has to have complete darkness and silence to sleep well whereas I am happier with some light and can sleep through a certain amount of noise (except that of a baby crying!).

It seems sensible to me to let his daytime naps be surrounded by family hustle and bustle but to reinforce the change to nighttime by keeping his bedroom reasonably quiet. There are some sounds, of course, that are very soothing to a sleeping baby, and I mention some of these on pages 62–65.

GETTING TO SLEEP

Many of the baby care books of twenty years ago or so recommended that the baby should be left in his crib to cry himself to sleep, and that if you went to him—or even worse, picked him up—you were "spoiling" him and setting a pattern that would never change. The experts nowadays, I am glad to say, nearly all agree that it is not possible to spoil a tiny baby, and that, far from teaching him bad habits by going to him when he needs you, you are equipping him with a sense of security and love that will last him all his life and make him all the more capable of giving love himself. There is of course a sort of settling-down-to-sleep fussing which a parent knows is not serious and will quickly stop, and it's certainly not a good idea to rush to the baby at the slightest sound, but any genuine distress should, I believe, be attended to. In many other cultures it is extremely rare to hear a baby cry, and it is odd that in our society we should have come to accept such an upsetting sound as part of everyday life. Certainly we seem to have been designed to respond quickly to it— there are very few commonly heard sounds at the same high frequency, and yet our hearing is particularly acute at that range. There may come a time when the baby is older when you have to let him complain for bursts of five minutes or so (see page 87), but in the early stages the more you go to him when he needs you the more independent he will be as a child.

Obviously it will not hurt the baby to be left occasionally for a few minutes to cry a little, since you certainly don't want to feel you have to let your entire life be dominated by his demands. But as a general rule, tiny babies cry because they need something or are unhappy. There can't be any hard and fast rules about such things, and finally it must remain an individual decision. Many parents do leave their babies to cry, and they grow up without any apparent ill effects, but I just find it impossible to listen to a young baby crying for any length of time without going to him.

A newborn baby will sleep whenever he needs to without any extra encouragement—usually right after a feeding—and will probably only awaken again when he is hungry. My three babies all followed the same pattern of sleeping for four to five hours at a stretch for the twenty-four hours after delivery and then changing to almost constant feedings for the next couple of days. Apart from making sure he is warm and comfortable for these first few days you can leave it entirely to your baby to drop off naturally at any time of day or night. After a few days, however, you may find that he needs a

"There's no law against pushing a carriage out at two in the morning."

little help to get peacefully off to sleep. If you are sure he's not hungry or in pain but he doesn't seem to settle in his bed, then your natural instinct will be to pick him up and cuddle him, which of course is exactly the right thing to do. After all, he's been used to complete security, warmth, and the soothing sounds and movement of your body for nine months, and to expect him to feel at home all on his own in a cradle may be asking too much of him. The ideal solution for the first few nights is to

51

take him into your bed, where he will fall asleep happily at your side after a feeding. (See page 33 for more about bringing him into your bed.) This may not suit you for any length of time, and in any case the baby will be sleeping much of the daytime to start with and for these naps may need to be helped to drop off on his own.

Also after the first few days, it's a good idea to encourage him to fall asleep without always having to be on the breast or sucking from a bottle, or later on you may find he has great difficulty getting to sleep without one of them and may continue waking in the night for "comfort feeds" when he's not really hungry. This can be a difficult habit to break.

POSITION

When you put him down in his bed you will have to decide for him whether he will sleep on his front or on his back. It will probably become clear quite quickly which he likes—usually on the front seems to be preferred. Research has shown that babies lying on their stomachs sleep longer than those on their backs, and of course if they should bring up small amounts of milk there is less danger of their choking. I like to vary the head position from side to side; in any case, by three months or so the baby will be able to turn it himself.

SWADDLING

One of the oldest ways of helping a baby to settle calmly into sleep is to swaddle him. The custom of swaddling is a very ancient one and until the eighteenth century was used in almost all societies. The baby was wrapped very tightly in bands of cloth so that the legs were kept together and the arms held by the sides. Then the baby was often strapped to a cradle board, which could be propped up or hung within sight and sound of the mother. We tend to think of this use of tight bands and cradle boards as cruel and inhibiting, but studies of cultures where it is still practiced, such as among the Navajo Indians, show that the babies are not kept this way all the time and that it undoubtedly calms and soothes them into sleep or into a quiet, alert state. Used sensibly, it does not hamper physical progress at all. Perhaps because they spend less time crying and more time calmly aware of their surroundings, if anything swaddled babies advance more quickly than unswaddled ones.

In our culture in recent years a form of semiswaddling has returned; in hospitals babies are frequently wrapped tightly in a cotton sheet before being tucked into their beds, and it's certainly worth pursuing this at home. A light woolen shawl or cellular baby blanket may be more effective than cotton, and since wool is slightly stretchy you are less likely to wrap him too tightly. Lay the baby on the shawl and gently wrap it around him, tucking the ends under his body to hold it in place.

For a newborn baby the arms are best wrapped by his sides, but if he still enjoys swaddling later on, bend his arms at the elbow and try to leave his forearms free, so that he can suck at his fingers if he likes.

"I would have given Katy fifty bright green pacifiers."

SUCKING

Some babies suck their fingers or thumbs at a very early age—there are even some who start in the womb. As long as it is not a constant habit it doesn't necessarily mean that the baby isn't being allowed long enough at the breast or bottle, and it can be a very comforting way for a baby to soothe himself to sleep. As long as you are sure you are feeding him enough and that he is allowed to suck at the breast long enough to keep up your milk supply, there is no reason why you shouldn't gently encourage his thumb into his mouth if he seems to want to go on sucking—it's certainly less tiring than having him constantly at the breast, which of course is really

54

what he's after. Certainly, research shows that, of those babies who are not always allowed to fall asleep at the breast, those who suck their thumbs or use a pacifier have on the whole less problem getting to sleep than those who don't. Some people are strongly against the use of pacifiers, but I found one invaluable for soothing my colicky daughter. The disadvantages are that they can easily get lost, that they may get dirty, and that they look rather unattractive, but these are unlikely to deter anyone who is really desperate to help a fretful, sleepless baby.

It's amazing how many preconceived ideas have to be abandoned once you have a baby. I had all sorts of theories about the upbringing of children, which very quickly bit the dust once I had real live ones of my own. Much against my original principles I would have given Katy fifty bright green pacifiers if it would have gotten her to sleep. There are times, such as when I find myself on Alexander's orders being a dump truck at six thirty in the morning, when I wonder if I've gone over a little too far to the enemy.

If used sensibly and not stuck in whenever the baby cries in place of food or cuddles, there's no doubt a pacifier can be very helpful in getting the baby to sleep, though never, of course, dipped in or filled with anything sweet. Sometimes he will wake again as soon as it falls out of his mouth, which can be quite a problem. If his cradle is next to your bed and you have a supply of clean pacifiers ready so you don't have to grope around in the dark looking for the lost one, this needn't be insurmountable. I don't like the idea of pinning or tying one onto the nightclothes, since however short the ribbon there is always the fear that it might catch around his neck or even just tangle uncomfortably in his fingers.

Apart from swaddling and sucking, the magic words to remember in getting a baby to sleep are *rhythm, move-*

ment, and *sound,* preferably all combined at the same time. None of these will work, of course, if the baby is hungry or uncomfortable, but once you are sure he has fed enough and is not wet, messy, or in pain, the following methods are worth trying.

RHYTHM AND MOVEMENT

One of the most natural ways of getting a baby to sleep is by rocking. It has been proven in experiments that gentle rocking at a rate of sixty to ninety rocks a minute will calm most babies. This corresponds of course to the heartbeat that the baby heard in the womb, and there is a natural instinct in most parents to pick up a crying baby and walk him around at a rate that will gently jog him up and down at just about that magic speed. Try putting him over your left shoulder—sometimes known as the "parrot position"—and pacing up and down. The left shoulder is said to be best because the baby can feel your heartbeat against him, but I suspect that it feels more natural for most of us because it leaves the right hand free.

If your baby brings up as much milk as my three you'll soon get used to all your clothes having rather unpleasant sticky marks on the left shoulders. I've never been efficient enough to always drape myself with a clean muslin square before carrying them. I find in any case that it's hopeless trying to look smart when bringing up young children—if it isn't spit-up on the shoulder then it's Play-Doh or paint all down my front.

If walking alone doesn't seem to help, try patting him quite hard on the back or bottom, as rhythmically as possible. Then try bouncing up and down while walking— rather uncomfortable but often effective. Sometimes going up and down stairs while holding the baby can achieve the same result; my sister and brother-in-law must have worn holes in their stair carpet while persuading their insomniac daughter to drop off to sleep.

A less tiring way of achieving the rate of sixty rocks a minute in an up and down movement is by using a Lullababy hammock (page 41). These are extremely successful in soothing babies to sleep and will save your time, energy, and temper. If you have several hooks in the house, you can pop the baby into one and carry on with getting the supper, getting the other children to bed, or just putting your feet up for a moment.

A baby sling or carrier is another good way of giving the baby the warmth, security, and movement he may be needing while leaving your arms free. There are various different types to buy, or you can make a sling out of a shawl or baby sheet, but I've never managed that very successfully. I found the sort that fasten with a simple clip at the back, with the baby positioned comfortably on my chest, the most effective. A carrier is extremely useful during the day for carrying the baby while shopping, cleaning, and so on. Since they often lull the baby to sleep they can also be used in the evening or nighttime in the house for a baby who needs lengthy walking to get him to sleep. I found that the baby had to be completely full before putting him in the sling, otherwise being so close to the food supply would remind him of that little bit of room he had left and he wouldn't be able to settle. Even when fully fed I found that the baby would sometimes protest for a few minutes when first put in, but as long as I kept walking briskly around the room—and even if necessary up and down the stairs or out of the front door and back again—he would soon go to sleep. Yes, I did get a few strange looks as I marched out onto the doorstep, danced around a bit in the fresh air and then disappeared back into the house again, but at the time that was the least of my problems. You may feel exhausted after having the baby in one for any length of time at first, but it's surprising how quickly your shoulders get used to the weight, and after a while you can more or less carry on with your evening routine as normal.

It's amazing how babies who like to be carried can sense the minute you sit down; even if you try to keep up the same rocking, jogging motion with your upper half, they seem to receive signals directly from your legs informing them the moment you should attempt anything as outrageous as trying to have a minute's rest. Occasionally a rocking chair can fool a baby like this— another old-fashioned but effective piece of equipment. Rocking gently to and fro with the baby on your shoulder, a drink in your hand, and a good book to read or television program to watch can be a very relaxing way of getting the baby to sleep. If he cries every time you put him down don't keep trying to force it; it will only end with both of you being frustrated and tired. Just let him sleep wherever he's comfortable—there will eventually come a moment later in the evening when you can sense that he's really deeply asleep enough to move him.

Some babies can be rocked to sleep in their own cradles, which of course is much easier. After having gone out of fashion for many years, there are now a few reasonably priced ones you can buy, and it's certainly worth trying one if your baby seems to like this sort of motion.

I didn't have one for Katy or Alexander, but while writing this book I have been trying Rory in a wooden swinging cradle during the day and it does seem to send him off to sleep beautifully. My sister-in-law in Los Angeles has a carry cot suspended in a frame, which can be wound up and then swings for forty-five minutes. It always gets her baby, Victoria Jane, to sleep. There are also the swing seats which are set in a very similar frame and also wind up. They're really meant for sitting in and swinging for fun, of course, but a friend of mine had a baby who could only be got to sleep in one of these: it was a bit tricky getting her out without waking her, but if she waited until the baby was deeply asleep she could just manage it. I've tried one at home and it does always send Rory to sleep and also seems to keep him happier when he's feeling a bit colicky in the evenings. I imagine pretty soon carry cots that swing will be more widely available, but until then the swing seat, although expensive, would be worth buying if you're really desperate. Perhaps a clever handyman could adapt the seat to make it easier to remove the sleeping baby.

Patting the baby on the back or side is another good thing to try—my own babies have all responded well to being patted firmly on the back in their beds while lying on their fronts. Katy seemed to need a sort of gentle shaking from a hand held firmly on her back, while Rory gets to sleep with a rhythmic patting on the bottom from one hand with the other one held firmly on his back. I even try to mimic the rhythm of a heartbeat with the bottom-patting hand, a sort of double beat every second or so. If that doesn't work, lifting the whole basket up and down in a rocking movement while still patting his bottom with the other hand will sometimes do it.

One mother told me that she was taught an ancient trick by an amah in Hong Kong: you hold the baby on his side on your lap and gently pat his thigh with your hand, keeping up a steady rhythm. She said that it worked wonders for her children and for those of her friends as well.

I have read several articles lately on "massaging" your baby. I can't honestly see that you need to learn any particular techniques, but of course the more physical contact you have with your baby the better, and a gentle rub with baby oil may well help to relax him and make

"The magic words in getting a baby to sleep are rhythm, movement *and* sound.*"*

him ready for sleep. Besides, it feels so lovely for both of you.

Some babies are sent off by the regular motion of a car, and many a parent has driven the streets in the middle of the night until his little insomniac finally succumbed. It's a very useful technique for daytime naps too, and for many years we have had to plan our trips in the car around children's sleep times—if you have to drive somewhere too late in the day then of course they are bound to drop off, and that means a bad night to follow. It generally works better with older babies and toddlers, but sometimes even tiny babies will respond. Strap the carry cot safely in the car and get your husband or a friend to drive so that you can sit in the back with the baby. Otherwise it can be very distracting for you to have the baby crying in the back and could be dangerous if you were tempted to keep turning around to see if he was all right. Older babies must of course be strapped safely in child seats in the back. There are now some new models that recline into sleeping positions.

Walking him out in the carriage in the fresh air is another good way of sending him off; the movement and change of atmosphere combined often settle a baby quickly, and there's no law that says you can't push a carriage out at two in the morning if necessary if it's not too cold. You may get some strange looks from passersby, but if you're finally getting the baby to sleep you won't care one little bit how peculiar you look. Children can drive one to do the most extraordinary things that soon become part of everyday life, and it's not until you look back that you realize just how odd some of your habits had become. For months I had to push Alexander around and around the block in his carriage at lunchtime, singing "Pop Goes the Weasel" in a very loud monotonous voice to get him off to sleep, and I used to get some very puzzled looks from the workmen on the scaffolding around the corner as I veered into view for the fourth and fifth time looking more and more desperate. Occasionally I would pass what was obviously a parent who understood, and I would feel his sympathetic and knowing glance.

If the carriage pushing works in the evening, it's probably best not to transfer the baby but to leave him to sleep in the carriage all night; some models have a top section which unclips from the wheels like a carry cot and can be carried into the bedroom. Or you can buy a set of wheels into which an ordinary carry cot will fit. You may not even need to wheel him outside; sometimes just a push around the room will do. If you live in an apartment you can keep his carry cot permanently on the wheels and give him a little push around every time he threatens to wake up.

SOUND

Singing to a baby is another very old method of soothing him—with all the rocking and patting ideas that I've mentioned it's worth trying some singing in his ear at the same time. Again, rhythm and monotony are the key. Lullabies are usually in a gently swinging sort of rhythm and the tunes also sound as if they rock up and down. Even if you feel you haven't the world's best singing voice it will sound wonderful to your baby—he'd rather have his mom or dad gently singing him to sleep than the greatest soprano in the world. There is also interesting recent research which shows that singing to a baby seems to be even more effective than just talking to him in terms of bringing on his ability to speak and become articulate. Mind you, as he grows older he may not appreciate your musical talents. I spent a good ten minutes the other night singing soothingly to a stony-faced

"As he grows older he may not appreciate your musical talents . . ."

Alexander, who finally looked me straight in the eye and said, "Yuk," very loudly and definitely. It didn't do much for any secret hopes I may have had of a singing career.

Some babies respond well to certain types of classical music, and it could be worth experimenting with some cassettes to see which particular composer your little one seems to favor.

Music boxes are also well worth trying. If you start using one above his cot every time you put him to bed the baby will sometimes learn to associate the sound with going to sleep and will drop off each night before the winding up runs out. You can buy mobiles that incorporate a music box, which hang over the cot and provide him with visual and aural stimulation at the same time. Make sure the mechanism keeps going for quite a long time before needing rewinding—it can be very frustrating if the music runs out just as the eyelids are getting heavy. A battery-run model could be better.

There are other sounds apart from music which can sometimes have a magic effect—regular, droning sounds such as that of a vacuum cleaner, hairdryer, or dishwasher, for instance. It's obviously not a very satisfactory way of regularly getting him to sleep, as presumably his bed is not that close to the dishwasher, and you certainly don't want to let yourself in for vacuuming his bedroom every night until he drops off. But they can be useful emergency measures for a fretful baby, and if he does like that kind of noise, it will at least give you a

"Some babies seem to respond well to certain types of classical music."

free pair of hands when you do want to dry your hair or use something mechanical. You must never of course leave any electrical appliance switched on near a baby while you are out of the room.

A more sophisticated and scientifically based version of the droning sound is the recently developed "womb music." Recordings were made inside a mother's womb of the gurgles, swishing, rumblings, and heartbeat that the baby would have heard while still inside, and it was found that playing these to crying babies would nearly always send them gently off to sleep. If started early enough, these recordings really do seem to work. I have a little corner at the back of my mind that rather puritanically feels that it's somehow just putting off the fact that the baby has to learn to live in the outside world and that we shouldn't fool him that he's still in the womb, but that's quite illogical really. It's only an extension of all the rocking and singing techniques, which are all to a certain extent mimicking life in the womb, and at any rate a desperate parent will quite rightly do anything to soothe a sleepless child. I was given a teddy bear with a cassette of womb music implanted in its tummy when Alexander was born—I did try to use it, but as he was so insatiably hungry for so much of his first few weeks I was never able to tell whether the womb music really helped or not, and by the time he was going for any reasonable length of time between feedings it was getting a bit late to start him on it. He does enjoy playing with it now—he carries it around, switching on and off the "funny noise." Who knows, perhaps even at two years three months he has a dim memory of life in the womb, and recognizes unconsciously the soothing sounds.

You can now buy cassettes of womb music and classical music combined, which seems a very good idea.

The older the baby gets the more important will routine become in ensuring peaceful bedtimes. After three or four months it's worthwhile trying to stick roughly to a regular bedtime and going through more or less the same ritual every night. This usually isn't something that has to be worked at; babies at around that age seem to slip into a fairly regular pattern of their own accord. The bedtime will probably be later at this stage than it will be as he gets older, but I think that's preferable to his being wide awake at four in the morning, ready for fun and games. Whatever time he seems ready to settle down for the night, stick to it, and go through more or less the same sequence of events. Set aside enough time to be able to bathe and dress him without having to rush, if that is your particular evening routine, and to be able to go through whatever singing, rocking, or patting ritual he seems to need. Put a cuddly toy or two in with him if you like—well away from his face, of course. If he grows to associate them with comfort and going to sleep happily it may make bedtime easier when he is older.

Try to accept the fact that he will take a specific amount of time to settle, and allow plenty. If you are always aware of how late it's getting and how you're never going to get the supper cooked/children to bed/house tidied up if you don't start soon, the baby will probably sense it and take even longer to get to sleep. If you can put him down and leave him while still awake, so much the better, but don't put yourself through miseries about it at this stage—I couldn't with any of mine when they were very small. Later on, as the baby gets older, being able to leave him will begin to matter much more, or you may find yourself hanging around for ages each evening until your toddler drops off.

MEDICINES

On the whole I am completely opposed to the use of medicines to get a baby to sleep, but there may very occasionally come a time when the parents and baby are so desperate and have got themselves into such a state that a doctor may feel justified in prescribing a mild sedative for a few days, usually an antihistamine, to try to help the family as a whole. If it works, the baby will not only sleep better while on the medication but with luck his sleep pattern will have been permanently changed. It is not a satisfactory solution, since apart from the distasteful idea of drugging a tiny baby, the sedative can occasionally work the opposite way to that intended, making the baby even more wakeful than usual. But it would be unrealistic to pretend that sedatives are not used by desperate parents; a surprisingly high percentage of babies are given them, and it is reasonable not to close one's mind to the possibility that their use may be necessary. I hope you will find a more natural answer to your baby's sleeplessness, even if it means waiting until he slips into a different pattern with time—and in any case, never give any medicine without your doctor's advice.

Herbs, on the other hand, have been used for centuries to calm babies and help them sleep, and the majority of them are completely safe. Whether they work is not fully established, but the following is a selection of the herbs which are claimed to help.

Anise
Used to be known as "Grandmother's gentle cure-all." Completely harmless, and the seeds made into a syrup are claimed to soothe babies.

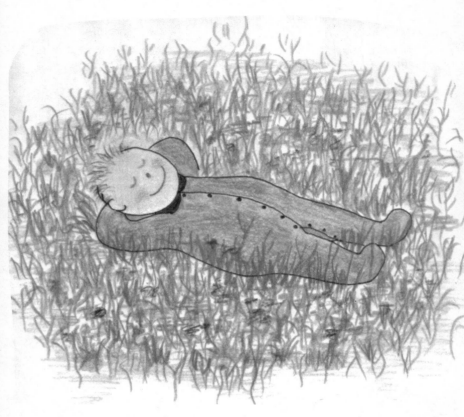

"Herbs have been used for centuries to calm babies."

Chamomile
Chamomile tea has been used as a calming, soporific drink for generations. They used to mix it with a little honey to administer it to babies.

Dill
"Dill procureth sleep," so Galen said. The name comes from a Saxon word meaning to lull, and dill water has

been used for this purpose for centuries. You can find
dill water in many health food stores.

Fennel
The Germans have used fennel to calm their babies for
many years. Fennel seed extract is available in health
food stores.

Mint
In Jamaica they give their babies mint tea to help them
sleep.

Alcohol
When I was at a particularly desperate pitch with Katy
not sleeping, someone recommended my giving her half
a teaspoon of sherry—she was up all night wide awake
and raring to go, obviously the type to be the life and
soul of the party in later years. Alcohol has been a
traditional treatment for colicky or fretful babies for
many years, but it's probably more useful for treating
the parents in most cases. For babies, I don't think it
should be encouraged, but for people who may be shocked
at the very idea it is interesting to note that the princi-
pal ingredient of many over-the-counter nostrums is
alcohol.

GETTING TO SLEEP SUMMARY CHART

Desperation Level	Have You Tried?	Page No.
One	Swaddling	53
	Thumb sucking	54
	Pacifier	55
	Herbs	67
	Rocking cradle	40
	Singing	62
	Music	63
	Lambskin	42
Two	Rocking chair	58
	Walking and rocking	56
	Going up and down stairs	56
	Droning	64
	Womb music	65
Three	Lullababy hammock	41
	Driving	61
	Taking a walk	61
Four	Doctor	67
Five	Alcohol	69
Six	Hammer!	—

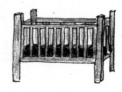

DISCOMFORT

There are many ways, of course, in which a baby can feel uncomfortable, and any one of them can be a factor in sleeplessness. You must try and eliminate all possible causes of irritation or pain before trying any of the ways of getting him to sleep, or your efforts will be wasted and you and the baby will end up very miserable.

GAS

We seem to have a bit of an obsession in our culture about gas. In some parts of the world they have never heard of burping their babies or getting the air out after feedings, and the babies don't appear to suffer any ill effects. But it does seem that many babies do feel discomfort if put in a lying position straight after a feeding, and in their case it's always best to get a good loud burp before attempting to get them to sleep. Methods vary in how to achieve this; with Alexander I found it easiest to

71

hold him on my lap with one hand supporting his chest and chin while my other hand gently rubbed his back and sort of squeezed the air up and out. With Rory it seems to work best with him slung over my left shoulder and patted firmly on the back. There's nothing more satisfying than getting up a really good dose of air, but you must avoid the temptation to blame everything on it. If a baby has been crying hard for some time, he will very likely have swallowed some air, and the fact that he brings some up (or down from the other end) doesn't necessarily mean that it was the original cause of the trouble. Experience will tell with your baby as to whether he always needs to be burped after a feeding, but if in doubt do it anyway—it's one less thing to worry about if he won't settle down.

COLIC

Colic is a term used to cover a variety of problems, which may or may not be connected with gas. Although some doctors would deny its existence, I believe true colic does occur and is a very real physical condition. My first two babies undoubtedly had it—at an early evening feed they would suddenly stop after a few sucks, pull up their legs, and scream violently and inconsolably. We suffered with them for a few days and then reluctantly gave them the antispasmodic drug that the doctor prescribed. It worked every well with both of them, although I found it difficult to give it to them the required fifteen minutes before a feeding, since babies fed on demand can be very unpredictable. Rory has been colicky in the evenings, but never badly enough to resort to using the drug. No doubt some would say that it was all due to tension in me and in the house in the evenings, and that with my third child I was more relaxed. I really don't think that was the cause, although my anxiety may well have exacerbated the problem. Anyone who has had a baby with bad colic will be extremely tense and anxious by the time they get to the doctor, and I think it can be very hard to be told that it may have all been caused by your tension and that you must relax or you will pass it on to the baby. Of course the baby senses your feelings, but I believe in most cases the colic precedes the tension. Why it is so often early evening that seems to be the worst time is unexplained—in my case I wondered if it was because I had less milk toward the end of the day—which I definitely did—but since bottle-fed babies also suffer evening colic, that can't be the full explanation. In any case, it seems very unsurprising that a tiny baby's intestines should take a few months to settle down, since they don't have to start working until after birth.

Whatever the cause, it can be a very miserable time for the whole family and any safe remedy is worth a try. Some breast-feeding mothers find that eliminating cow's milk in any form from their own diets seems to help, suggesting that colic can be caused by an allergy to cow's milk protein. If you are going to try this you must do it rigorously, there's no point in half measures since, if the theory is correct, even the smallest trace of cow's milk in your diet will spoil the whole experiment. Cut out butter, milk, cheese, and yogurt, and read the list of ingredients in everything you eat—for instance, many crackers contain whey powder. You can buy goat's milk and goat's milk products in many supermarkets now, or try one of the new soy milks. Beware of the soft margarines—many of these contain milk products. Salt-free, no-cholesterol corn oil margarines—Fleischmann's for example—usually do not. Keep to this diet strictly for a week or two, and if you don't find any improvement, give it up. It didn't seem to help either of mine, but in my sister Clare's case it worked very well, and some

73

"Some medicines unfortunately taste really disgusting."

people report quite dramatic improvements. It's difficult to prove that it is really the mother's diet that is the cause, since colic can come and go so suddenly in any case, and no mother is going to experiment with going off the diet just to prove a point.

Other foods eaten by the mother are often blamed for causing colic, and at one time or another I must have been told or read that almost everything edible can be guilty. Nuts, chocolate, grapes, cabbage, alcohol, spicy foods, plums, apples, etc. etc. There's no doubt that certain foods do seem to upset certain babies, and it's always worth cutting out something you are suspicious of to see if it helps—too much caffeine from drinking tea or coffee in large quantities goes straight through to the baby, for instance. Also, for a breast-feeding mother it is wise to eat regularly throughout the day and not save up for a large evening meal. For a bottle-fed baby it is worth asking your doctor about changing the formula, perhaps to a soy-based one.

Sometimes a colicky baby seems to confuse his tummy pains with hunger, and he will try to feed to soothe himself—if it works, all well and good. A few extra feedings will not hurt, especially if he's breast-fed. If, however, he gulps very fast and fills himself with air he may well make himself worse, and this is the time to try a pacifier. Some people object to these, but if it makes the baby feel better it's worth it every time, even if you only use it for his colicky patches in the evening. If he is bottle-fed, a smaller hole in the nipple can sometimes help, by slowing down the speed at which he takes the milk. A friend of my sister's had very sore nipples and got hold of a British National Childbirth Trust shield. She breast-fed very comfortably that evening and the baby seemed very contented. It wasn't for several hours that she discovered the shield had no hole in it—they leave you to make your own to the required size.

There are some wonderfully cheering pieces of research into almost every aspect of child care: a good morale booster is that colicky babies are said to be more common in mothers of higher intelligence. The fact that I have had two with severe colic and a third without presumably confirms that depressing statistics about brain cells dying off as you get older—certainly when faced with Katy's math homework I feel as if they've all given up the ghost already.

"The heartbeat that the baby would have heard while still inside."

The important thing to remember about colic is that it will pass; perhaps not at the magic three-month milestone so often quoted, but certainly fairly soon after that. It is a wretched thing for parents and babies, but it will be grown out of and will not remain a permanent block to getting to sleep.

DIAPERS AND CLOTHING

The comfort of diapers and clothing is something to check very carefully. If you use cloth diapers, make sure they are very soft. Rinse out every trace of laundry detergent and use a fabric conditioner. For disposable users, make sure you buy the brand that best suits the baby's shape and size and that doesn't feel too sharp-edged and "crunchy" to you. Take care, too, that you never stick the little tabs to any of his skin by mistake. His undershirt also must feel nice and soft—babies' skin is very delicate and can be chafed uncomfortably very easily. Check baby's pajamas, nightgown or sleeper for roughness, tightness, rubbing labels, and so on—remember, there's no way that the baby can tell you what may be bothering him. When I was about one and a half my father apparently spent a whole day with me whining and complaining inarticulately only to discover at bedtime that he had put both of my legs through one hole in my underwear when dressing me that morning.

DIAPER RASH

This can be a common cause of wakefulness. If it's bad you must consult your doctor; it may be caused by something needing specific treatment. But there are some things you can do to avoid the common rashes. Change the diaper as frequently as possible and always as soon as the baby has passed a stool. Use a disposable one-way

77

liner, which will help to keep the skin dry. Leave the diaper off as much as possible to let air get to the skin. Clean the skin thoroughly every time you change him, but preferably not with soap and water, which can be very drying. Johnson's Baby Bath is a good substitute. If you use that you will not need anything else, but if you clean with a simple baby lotion rub in a little protective cream afterwards. Don't use plastic pants if there is any hint of soreness. At any sign of a rash apply plenty of one of the many special creams. If it doesn't improve very quickly, consult your doctor and work hard together to get rid of it—a baby with a sore bottom is naturally going to be unhappy and unable to sleep well.

Breast-fed babies are less likely than bottle-fed to get diaper rash, but they are in no way immune to it. Especially when you start to introduce solids into the baby's diet and the stools change, you must be prepared for the possibility of a reaction in the skin around his bottom.

Some disposable diapers may be whitened with a chemical which could possibly cause a reaction in the skin of certain babies, and it's a good idea to stick with a brand that is not treated in this way. Some are also perfumed and "sanitized." Both perfume and antiseptic can cause problems in some babies. Check the label for a type which is free from any bleach or chemical.

If he gets very wet at night and you don't want to have to keep waking him up to change him, slip an extra disposable pad inside his usual diaper.

Most babies dislike being left in a messy diaper, so if he passes a stool in the middle of the night you will have to change him. With any luck his body will adapt fairly quickly to a daytime pattern and at night the diapers will be only wet.

ECZEMA

Another type of rash that is quite often found in babies is infantile eczema. This can cause very bad itching and keep the poor baby awake. Of course, you will consult your doctor immediately if you find any patches and follow whatever treatment he prescribes. One comfort is that this type of eczema is usually grown out of by the time the child is two.

COLDS

Colds are also frequently causes of difficulty in sleeping, particularly in a northern winter. If the baby's nose gets very blocked up he may be unable to feed. This will distress him and make him cry, which in turn will make his nose even worse, and you are into a difficult vicious circle. Your doctor may prescribe nose drops to use before feeding, but of course you should avoid using them for any length of time. Try Vicks Vapo Rub in a vaporizer. If he tends to get a cough whenever he gets a cold, it may be worth buying a humidifier. The most effective but expensive kind are those that puff out a stream of cool mist—healthier for babies than old-fashioned hot steam. If you suspect that the baby has a temperature or may have pain in his ears or throat, you must seek medical help quickly; an infection must be dealt with straightaway. Ear trouble, unfortunately, seems to be only too common in young children, but as long as it is attended to correctly it is something they will grow out of without being left with any damage. Make sure he is not getting either too hot or too cold in the night (see pages 42, 45, and 48 for suggestions for bedding, clothes, and room temperature).

TEETHING

The pain of teething seems to affect babies in very different ways—some sail through the whole business unscathed while others have a very miserable time. It is dangerous to blame too much on teething, and you should always check with the doctor if there is any fever, ear rubbing or bad diaper rash—just three of the many symptoms that some mothers remain convinced are part of the normal teething process. However, it can make the gums very sore and cause extra drooling, which in turn may produce a rash around the mouth, and it is a very common cause of waking in the night.

There are various remedies you can try, one of which may work for your particular baby. There are gels and lotions to rub on the sore gum with your finger, which do help to numb the area temporarily and may relieve the pain long enough for the baby to be able to get back to sleep. Be wary of using these too much, since they contain local anaesthetics, which can occasionally cause allergies, and some of them also contain aspirin. They appear to taste delicious—Katy was a real teething gel freak and even now will use every excuse to be allowed to use it. I never realized the second set of teeth coming through could cause such problems. An old remedy is simply firm and rhythmic rubbing with the thumb or finger while the baby is being cuddled. Not so good at night—though if Mom or Dad is awake anyway they might as well do it. A teething ring or very hard cookie to bite on may bring relief, but of course only use them while you are there—never leave the baby alone in his bed with something in his mouth. Put things that he likes to bite on in the refrigerator; often the coldness can bring a little extra relief.

Some of the homeopathic and herbal remedies are safely worth a try—for instance, there is a chamomile

preparation that you rub onto the gums and tongue which is said to bring relief.

If the teething is very bad a little children's aspirin or Tylenol may be necessary to relieve the pain—but remember, there will be lots of teething to come, and you don't want to be reaching for the aspirin bottle every time it appears.

Older babies may continue to wake in the night even once the teething bout is over, and you may have to gently break them of the habit (page 84).

MEDICINES

As a general rule I am against the use of medicines to help a baby sleep except in very special circumstances, but obviously if the baby is unwell there may be a need for their use. The golden rule is never to give any form of medicine without medical advice. If the baby has an itchy condition such as eczema or urticaria, the doctor may prescribe a mild sedative to help him sleep, usually an antihistamine. Naturally, this should be used for as short a time as possible. If he is in pain or running a temperature, on your doctor's advice you may need to give him a little children's aspirin or Tylenol. If he is prescribed an antibiotic to combat an infection be sure he finishes the complete prescription.

Some medicines unfortunately taste really disgusting,

and the sweet flavorings used in an attempt to mask them don't always help. Alexander recently had to undergo a course of antibiotics for an ear infection and took violently against the bright pink liquid containing it. Getting him to take it three times a day became a battle, and it was heartrending for us to have to administer it to a protesting but still polite two-year-old screaming "No thank you!" as we approached him with the spoon. Still, of course, it was worth it in the end to see him free of the ear-rubbing misery he had been in.

There has been much interest in alternative medicine in recent years, and there are homeopathic and herbal remedies that can safely be tried.

OLDER BABIES AND TODDLERS

Much of the preceding chapters will apply to babies of all ages, but there are also additional and very different problems and solutions that arise once the baby has dropped his night feedings and begins to grow into more of an independent person.

FEEDING

The age at which he will stop waking from hunger will vary considerably. Some wonderful morning you may wake up and realize with amazement that you have slept right through the night. It can be quite a startling experience—the first time Katy slept right through I woke in a panic thinking something was wrong. Don't, however, be fooled into thinking the baby will never wake in the night again; often you get one or two good nights followed by another bad one. With luck the good ones will become more frequent, until it is rare to be awakened for a feeding.

If this happy course of events doesn't happen naturally there are one or two ways of trying to encourage it. If you find you are being regularly awakened an hour or so after you get into bed it may be worth waking the baby for a feeding just before you go to sleep. At least then you will get the full benefit of the next stretch between feedings, and with any luck he will go that bit longer than he would have otherwise, since he will be completely topped up. If you are convinced that he is waking in the night more from habit than from hunger it may be worth giving him warm boiled water instead of his feeding—with some babies, after a few nights this seems to persuade them that it is not worth their while waking up. It's probably better if Dad goes to him at night if you are trying to drop a feeding; the smell of milk on the mother may remind him of feeding when he doesn't really need it.

Follow the advice in Feeding on making the night feedings as quick, boring, and uneventful as possible.

If he still continues to wake, take a feeding, and go back to sleep again, just accept the fact that he still needs it, and count yourself lucky that at least you still have an easy way of getting him quickly back to sleep.

Breast-fed babies may go on taking feeds at night well into their second year and you should never feel that you are in any way doing something wrong or "spoiling" them by continuing to give it to them.

BEDTIME

The older the baby gets the more important routine becomes in helping him to settle happily to sleep. If from an early age it is an accepted fact of life that at a certain time each evening he will have a bath followed by some quiet play and then be tucked into bed for a few songs and a good-night kiss, or whatever ritual may have evolved, it will be much easier for him to feel secure about being left to go to sleep. There will come a time, of course, in many toddlers' lives when they suddenly realize that they don't after all have to do everything you say without question, and there are bound to be some protests about bed at some point. Alexander can produce some magnificent tantrums, and as he's a big strong baby we have sometimes had to go through some ferocious wrestling matches on the way up to bed. I suppose I like to think of myself as a peace-loving liberal, and it's quite startling to have produced a little creature who can turn into an aggressive furious monster hurling heartfelt if limited epithets at his devoted mother. Having been through that a few times, though, he soon found it didn't cut any ice, and he's now very happy to go to bed each evening. Katy used to protest on occasion just as violently in her own way, but at least it was more vocally than physically.

Of course, in times of illness or on a special occasion, such as a birthday or a visit from a grandparent, the rules will be broken, but on the whole the more the bedtime routine can be stuck to the happier everyone will be.

Never, never use bed as a threat during the day. You can't expect him to go happily up to his bedroom at night if he has been told he'll be "sent to bed" when doing something naughty.

If as a small baby he has always dropped off to sleep while feeding, you may have to gently and gradually teach him to fall asleep in his crib. Try some of the ideas on pages 49–70. If you find you are spending hours every night singing, rocking, or patting, a consistent program of kind retraining may be necessary.

As soon as possible, you want to get into the habit of leaving the room with him still awake but happy, rather than hovering around waiting for him to fall asleep. Talk about a watched pot never boiling—my husband and I between us must have spent countless hours sitting next to Katy's crib watching her eyelids droop into apparent slumber over and over again. It's amazing how long children can fight sleep when they really want to. My uncle Harry had a theory that by standing at the head of the crib instead of the side he could make my cousin drop off more quickly; the strain of tilting the head up and back to look at his father would help the eyes to close sooner. No success guaranteed, but an interesting idea.

Check the room for any pictures or objects that may look "spooky" in the half dark and be worrying the child into staying awake—coats on backs of doors, paintings with faces, and so on. Beware of this being played on once they can talk: my little niece Sarah would keep her father in the bedroom for hours by calling him back over and over again as she found new things that were "worrying" her—"Oh, and Daddy, that picture there . . . and I think that book on the table looks a bit funny . . . and those curtains are rather strange. . . ." she practically had the room cleared each night, until Dad put his foot down.

Don't make the change from day to night too sudden; try to wind down the excitement level gradually to aim toward a calm bedtime. Make the late afternoon games gentle ones, and try to avoid confrontation in the prebed hours. It's worth ignoring small misdemeanors rather than end the day with a fight. A warm drink of milk can sometimes help make him sleepy. Put it in a bottle if he still enjoys the comfort of sucking.

Once he's in bed and you have finished the ritual, try puttering around where he can still hear you, tidying up or putting out his clothes for the next day and perhaps even quietly chatting to him while you do it, until you casually mention that you're going downstairs now or into the kitchen to make Daddy's supper, etc.

One evening when I wasn't feeling very well I told Alexander as I left the room that I was going to put on my night things and get ready for bed. He happened to go off to sleep very easily and peacefully, and so I said it again the next night, and the next, until I found myself in the ludicrous position of having to put a dressing gown over my clothes each evening when I went back to tuck him in so as not to be caught out if he should awaken.

My niece used to go to sleep happily if my sister said she was just "running out to use the bathroom," so every night for months that's what she said. Little Helen must surely have wondered why on earth her mother never remembered to go before she put her to bed.

Don't let it always be the same parent that puts him to bed—it will make life much easier if from an early age either Dad or Mom can do the bedtime routine.

Never be tempted to get the baby out of bed or you will find it very difficult to get him back again, and he will bully you every evening until you get him out.

By now he may well have adopted a comfort object, whether it's a favorite toy, blanket, or pacifier, or just a well-sucked thumb: many children use such things as an indispensable part of their nighttime routine. Never try to discourage this—it's all part of the process of learning to comfort himself and to sleep without your presence, and research shows that children who have such habits have far fewer problems with getting to sleep than those without. If you can engineer it so that the chosen object is easily duplicated you may save yourself a lot of trouble later. Many parents have spent frantic evenings searching for some beloved one-eared moth-eaten bunny without which the protesting toddler adamantly refuses to go to sleep. Put a couple of books or safe toys in the crib that he can play with on his own before he goes to sleep.

If in spite of all this careful preparation for sleep he still cries when you leave the room, wait a few minutes, go back, give him another kiss and cuddle, tuck him in again, say good night firmly, and *leave*. You may have to repeat this over and over again the first few nights, but as long as you keep going back as cheerfully as possible he will eventually realize that you are never far away and that you are not leaving him forever and he will settle down to sleep. He may scream and shout each time you leave the room, but if you keep calm and go back each time after a few minutes it will be more out of anger than distress. Never leave him unhappy for long— five minutes is the absolute maximum—and never give in and take him out of bed or you will be going right back to square one. This may well take an hour or more of going in every few minutes, but if you don't weaken it will eventually work and after two or three days will get shorter and shorter. I believe a toddler likes the security of knowing you will stick to what you say, as long as it is done kindly. If he has got into the habit of a prolonged bedtime with you staying in the room until he is asleep, be sure to set aside a few free evenings to begin your new routine; if you are worrying about cooking supper or getting on with something downstairs it will make it much harder for you to spend much of the evening going in and out of his room every five minutes without getting very tense.

Never leave him to cry alone in his bed for long—even if it eventually "trains" him to go to sleep on his own, you will have put him through some extremely lonely and unhappy times and taught him that he is right to feel insecure about your love and attention.

If he is a child who needs very little sleep you may have to keep him up all evening until you go to bed. This is the standard practice in many parts of the world; we are in the minority in expecting to have child-free evenings. I must say I rather value them—they seem to be the only times my husband and I manage to sustain uninterrupted conversations.

DAY BEFORE

It is very unfair to expect a baby to go happily to sleep at night if he is just not tired. It is up to you to make sure that he has had the right amount of daytime activity and sleep to suit his particular needs, and to leave him tired enough to sleep but not overtired. Make his days as enjoyably exhausting as possible; include active physical exercise, preferably in the fresh air, as well as plenty of intellectual stimulation.

As he gets older you will have to become more aware

of how much sleep your particular baby needs and adjust his daytime naps so that he is tired enough at night. Babies vary so much in the amount they need that it is important to predict a set pattern, but at some stage you will notice that the haphazard routine of the early days will settle into morning and afternoon naps. If necessary you will have to wake him from the afternoon early enough for him to be ready for bed later on. Never let him drop off in the late afternoon—it may be tempting after a long demanding day to get a few minutes peace, particularly as this can be the most fractious time, but you will regret it later. Keep him awake by any means possible, so that he will be ready for a peaceful bedtime and a good night's sleep. A walk in the carriage or stroller or a drive in the car too late in the day may be fatal—many's the time I've had to lift a drowsy child out of the stroller and carry it home on one arm, chatting or making silly faces at it in order to keep it awake, with the other arm trying to manage stroller, shopping, and an irritable eight-year-old.

There will come an awkward stage when two daytime naps are too much and one is not quite enough. You will just have to play it by ear, letting him have the two rests when he is really tired and then perhaps managing two or three days with only one. The pattern will be entirely an individual one and only you can judge how much sleep he needs during the day without spoiling his nights.

Whatever pattern of daytime sleep you find he needs, stick to it. Don't be tempted to let him sleep on in the afternoon, for instance, if you know he has had enough; wake him gently. Alexander always woke in the most terrible mood from his afternoon nap and the rest of the family had to steel itself for the onslaught of "Yuck," "Go away," "You're horrible," etc., etc., with which the waker would be greeted (his early grasp of language did have its disadvantages), but we knew the penalty of

89

"Try to avoid confrontation in the prebed hours."

leaving him to sleep peacefully on would have to be paid later.

Eventually he will be ready to drop the daytime naps altogether, but be prepared for him to need it occasionally, especially after a particularly active morning or when he has been ill. Once he starts in a play group or nursery school he may return to an after-lunch snooze on a regular basis for a while.

Don't try to make him drop the daytime naps too early by forcing him to stay awake all day long—you might think that it will make him so tired that he will sleep better at night, but it just doesn't work that way. Overtiredness is just as destructive to good peaceful sleep as not being tired enough. There have been several occasions when I have let one of the children have a longer and later nap during the day than I intended and have anticipated a difficult bedtime and wakeful night, only to be taken quite unawares by one of the longest and quietest nights ever. You can never safely predict which will be the perfect amount of sleep during the day, but on the whole you can normally judge it fairly well.

Once daytime naps have been dropped on a fairly regular basis, you may find he needs an earlier bedtime to compensate. The thought of an extra hour without his company in the evening may not fill you with too much dismay, now that you are looking after him all day without the accustomed break while he sleeps. . . .

Try to avoid any stressful situations during the day until his sleeping is more consistent. Any major change in his life may well be reflected in his nighttime behavior. You may find yourself delaying moving house until he's in his twenties. . . .

Traveling with a child who sleeps badly can be very difficult, but equally they can sometimes surprise you with their reactions: occasionally a change of scene seems to throw them into a better sleeping pattern. A friend of mine had a sleepless child who slept through the night for the first time on a visit overseas—the jet lag seemed to take her so by surprise that it mixed up her whole schedule and reset it into a much calmer and longer-sleeping one. It continued after they returned home. Unfortunately, it would be somewhat impractical and expensive to send sleepless children on international flights at government expense, but it does illustrate just how complicated and unpredictable the whole business is.

Try to see that he eats well during the day so that he will not wake in the night through hunger. As with little babies, it's more a question of his input taken as a whole than a large meal just before bed.

Avoid stories or television programs that may inspire bad dreams, often the cause of a child's waking at night. It's sometimes difficult to foretell what may be the cause of worrying thoughts, but if you do get a hint that something may upset him don't try to tease him out of it. The fear may seem quite irrational to you but it is very real to him, and if he feels you don't understand he may keep it hidden inside where it may easily emerge in nightmares.

WAKING IN THE NIGHT

Once the baby is no longer waking to be fed in the night, you of course hope that he will consistently sleep right through. Unfortunately this is frequently not the case, and the toddler who still wakes his parents two or three times in the night is far more common than many people think.

Most babies wake in the night several times, but it depends on what they do when they wake as to whether it is seen as a problem. If they turn over and go straight back to sleep then of course no one will even be aware that they have awakened. If, on the other hand, they cry for company and refuse to go back to sleep for several hours it can become a very real problem indeed.

First check for any physical discomfort that may be waking him (see Discomfort). If he kicks off his covers in the night and gets cold, put him into one of the cozy all-in-one sleep suits, or fix the blankets with clips to the rails and the crib. Alexander always slept better if I turned his quilt sideways and tucked it firmly around him under the mattress—acting perhaps as a sort of toddler swaddling as well as keeping him warm. If necessary, put a heater in the room in very cold weather. If you think he gets too hot put him in thinner nightwear or leave the window open wider; there is much less danger from getting too cold once the baby is six months or so.

Make sure the room is neither too light nor too dark—fear of the dark is very real and should not be dismissed or laughed at. If you live in an old creaky house, as we do, you will need to work out the most silent route for entering and leaving the baby's room in the night. If he is waking just as you go to bed each evening, consider

93

whether you are making unnecessary noise that may be disturbing him—during shallow periods of sleep even a distant toilet flushing may get through to him. Do you have central heating that is on an automatic timer that may be making a noise as it switches itself off?

If you have checked for all physical causes but he still continues to wake in the night, it is obviously for some less easily solved reason. I have never been able to leave a baby or child crying on his own in the night—if it eventually did stop him calling I've always felt it would have been a battle won at far too high a price. On the other hand, some parents find that ignoring their babies' cries in the night for a few days can quickly break a habit of waking. If you and the neighbors can stand it, it may be something to try if you're desperate and is certainly nothing to feel guilty about. If you're not prepared to ignore him, one solution is to bring him into your bed in the middle of the night. This will give him the security and comfort he is after and may give all of you the chance to get quickly back to sleep. The trouble is that once you start doing it, it will be very difficult to stop again without causing much misery, so unless you are prepared to have him sleeping in the bed with you for quite some time to come it's probably best avoided. Also, some toddlers turn into windmills as soon as they hit the sheet, or else manage to produce more extraordinary variations on the sound of breathing than you would think possible from such tiny noses and mouths. (See page 35 for more on the family bed.) There will be times when he is unwell when you will naturally want to bring him into bed for a cuddle, but unless it is to become a regular habit, once he is better you must make it clear that it is time to go back into his own bed.

A compromise is to bring his bed into your bedroom. You may find that he sleeps much better knowing that you are near all night, and even if he does wake up

"By now he may well have adopted a comfort object."

95

you may be able to calm him merely by the sound of your voice.

Alternatively you can put a camp bed temporarily in his bedroom, so that if necessary you can spend the night in his room. This means that at least one parent will get a good night's sleep, and if you put the extra bed right next to his bed, a reassuring pat may be enough to quiet him. If you have other children in the family you could try putting the toddler in with them. You might think they would all end up waking, but surprisingly enough this doesn't usually happen, and quite often the feeling of there being someone else in the room helps the wakeful one to sleep through the night. After all, most humans in the world even today sleep with their young, and we are unusual in expecting them to sleep alone.

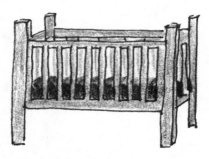

Unless he is ill or extremely upset by some event of the day it's not a good idea to take him out of bed and bring him downstairs or into your living room. We made the mistake of doing just that with Alexander, who soon got into the habit of regular four thirty A.M. games and fun. It took a long time to break him of the habit and would have been much better never started in the first place. The "cure" consisted of sitting with him in the early hours, kindly but firmly refusing to take him out of bed. He did get very upset, but I felt that as long as one of us was with him, usually holding him in a tight cuddle and singing or chatting to him while still in his bed, he would not feel any loneliness or real distress. After a lot of protests he would eventually lie down and then after a good-night kiss and a tuck-in we would leave the room. This sequence had to be repeated a few times for the first two or three nights, but he then learned that it was a waste of time to keep it up and accepted that he was going to be in bed all night.

If he wakes and you don't want to start playing musical beds, go to him right away, reassure him, kiss him good-night, and *leave*. If he cries, go back after a minute or two and repeat this, being kind and loving but firmly letting him know that night is for sleeping and that you're not going to get involved in any long sessions with him. Consistency and firmness are vital. You may have to repeat this several times for a few nights, but he will eventually realize that you mean what you say, and thereafter even if he does awaken he will probably go quickly back to sleep again.

If he's thirsty give him water, not sweet interesting drinks.

Be firm but kind in the night; try not to lose your temper with him but equally don't get involved in long rocking or singing sessions or you will be doing it every night.

If he climbs out of his crib, take him firmly back and settle him down again. The more quickly you do this the better, so that he learns it's not worth his while to try. If you have always responded quickly to his cries he may never have tried this anyway.

Some children will play happily on their own in the night if they wake—you could try putting a couple of safe toys or books in the corner of his crib. If he always wants a drink when he wakes up then a beaker with a lid could also be put in the corner of the crib; he might just learn to help himself without disturbing you.

Something well worth trying if a consistent pattern of night waking exists is to get someone else to put the baby to bed for a few days. With several wakeful toddlers I know this had quite a dramatic effect on their sleeping. It's probably best if the parent who usually puts them to bed actually leaves the house as if to go out—or even goes away for a few days—leaving the toddler with the other parent or someone else whom he trusts. This very often stops them from waking: it's as if they sense that it's not worth their while calling as Mom/Dad isn't there. A few days of this may set a new pattern.

Sometimes star charts used in the morning can be effective. Let him stick on his own star every time he sleeps right through the night. This is known by behavioral psychologists as "reinforcement"; in other words, when they do something good something nice happens. It's a new name for a very old technique for dealing with people—bribery—and one to which most of us invariably resort.

If he wakes with what they call "night terrors," there's nothing you can do but help him through them. Katy occasionally had them. They are different from nightmares in that the child is neither asleep nor fully awake, but in a strange confused state of fear which may take a few minutes to subside. You can't really get through to him and it's best just to cuddle him and talk reassuringly until it's over.

The same method applies to dealing with nightmares, but it's worth thinking through the events of the preceding day or so to discover any obvious cause—a frightening program on television or an overly realistic game of monsters, perhaps. There may be some problem or change in his life which is making him insecure. Children can be anxious over apparently minor problems that nevertheless are overwhelmingly important to them. You may need to gently wake him from his nightmare before he can allow himself to get back to peaceful sleep.

Never leave a child alone with a night terror or nightmare. He is not "taking advantage" but needs you to calm him. Let him have a light left on in the room if it reassures him, or a door left ajar with a light on the landing.

WAKING EARLY

Waking early when you have a baby becomes part of your life, but it all depends what you mean by early as to whether you find it bearable or not. To us, after three early risers, anything after six is tolerable, after seven very reasonable, and after eight unimaginable luxury.

Parents of young children are in a strange category all their own when it comes to the twice yearly time changes, reacting in quite the opposite way to the rest of the population. When the clocks go forward for summertime, for most "normal" people it means they are deprived of an hour's sleep: for you and me it means the baby will be waking—oh joy!—at six thirty rather than five thirty. And at the return of standard time, when most people enjoy an extra hour in bed, we can only look forward to baby's return to waking at some unearthly hour.

There are ways of trying to give yourself a few extra precious minutes:

If light is waking him in the summertime put up heavier curtains or line the present ones with dark material.

As long as he sleeps within earshot put a beaker of drink and a zwieback next to the bed where he can

reach them. With these plus a couple of interesting toys he might amuse himself for a little while.

If a wet or messy diaper wakes him, you might find that after a change and a cuddle he will play on his own and let you go back to bed for a while.

If there is an older child in the family, let him go to the baby when he wakes. They may easily learn to keep each other company in the mornings.

Make sure you're not putting him to bed too early—it may be preferable to have his company for a little longer in the evenings than to be awakened horribly early.

Take turns with your husband being the one to go to him in the mornings, so that at least one parent will get some sleep.

Try to see things through your child's eyes: it can sometimes be very difficult to guess what may be affecting them. One little boy I knew, having always been happy to play in his crib in the early mornings, suddenly started getting very upset when he awoke. The parents went through everything that might be worrying him, clearing the room of everything he might see first thing that could be causing his distress. It wasn't for a long time that they realized that on the mantel-piece was a postcard from Wales: on the postcard was a stamp: on the stamp was a dragon!

Make the most of early morning television; sometimes even the news and weather can be fascinating enough for a baby for you to be able to doze off for a few moments on the sofa. I must say though that there is something rather depressing about finding yourself waiting impatiently for Good Morning America at 6:15 in the morning. Sundays are wonderful, of course, if one is lucky enough to get that full hour of relief of *Sesame Street* in the morning.

Finally, accept early waking as another of those aspects of parenthood that are regrettable but unavoidable; try to get to bed at a reasonable hour while the phase lasts, and above all, enjoy your lively loving baby at what can be one of his most charming times—all warm, sleepy, and tousled, and ready to give you a heart-melting smile. (Except our Alexander, who tends to wake up unbelievably grumpy and ready for battle, and like many adults has to be handled very tactfully for the first few minutes. The aim is to avoid all confrontation until he has had his cornflakes, after which he begins to be more like his usual jolly self.)

HOW TO COPE

Asleepless baby can disrupt the entire household. Particularly, of course, one or both of the parents will suffer, as lack of sleep in itself is extremely debilitating, quite apart from the trauma of pacing the floor with a wakeful, crying baby. It is very important that you think of yourself and your partner occasionally and that you don't let the baby entirely dominate your lives. It is to be hoped that both mother and father will be equally involved in every aspect of looking after the baby; love and support for each other can be vital during these difficult nights.

There is a natural tendency in the middle of the night to blame someone or something for one's lack of sleep, and as your husband or wife is usually the person within firing range the most enormous amount of resentment can be built up. I've known nights when we've been up with one of the babies when I've so much wanted to shout at someone that I've almost unconsciously tried to engineer a situation in which an argument could be started. In our house we have always shared the night vigils as equally as breast-feeding will allow, but it obviously makes sense to alternate nights to a certain extent so that at least one of you gets some sleep. In spite of the logic of there being no point in two of you being kept awake, there is something supremely irritating about a snoring spouse lying in bed while mother or father paces the floor with the baby. It can be one of the loneliest times of all, and at three in the morning when you are at your lowest ebb you can begin to feel that the whole world is against you.

My sister used to keep a diary of her bad nights with her daughter; she found it helped to write down some of the despairing thoughts she used to have. Part of the trouble is that as well as the awful tiredness and unhappiness you can feel enormous guilt: here you are with a healthy baby, complaining about something as trivial as lack of sleep. It certainly isn't trivial at the time, and anyone who has gone through years of being awakened regularly at night from deep sleep, possibly to be kept up for hours at a stretch, will know just what an insidious form of torture it can be.

Probably the most important thing to remember is that it will pass. It's hard to realize it, but there will come a time when the children will all sleep through the night and will even resent your getting them up in the morning, and the more love and attention you have given them in the early years, particularly at night, the more loving and secure people they will themselves grow up to be. If you think of every time you go to them at night as a sort of premium in an insurance policy, which will pay out for the whole of their adult lives, it makes it easier to bear.

As you've crept out of the room after apparently settling your little angel for the twelfth time and he screams for Mommy or Daddy just as you are finally sitting

103

down to your dried-up lukewarm supper, try to keep any unavoidable swearing out of his earshot. Many's the time I've muttered the most hideous oaths silently to myself as I return for the umpteenth time to the baby's room, and it takes the performance of a lifetime to enter sweetly and lovingly once more into the monster's lair.

Parents whose children sleep through the night from an early age are very lucky, but you must never let them make you feel that the fact that yours still wake in the night at the age of two or three is in any way your fault or anything particularly unusual. More than twenty percent of babies are still waking regularly at a year old or beyond. There is evidence to show that the type of alert, wakeful infant that doesn't sleep through the night for a long time will have been in some way programmed to be so since birth, or even from midpregnancy, so there is no reason to suppose that it is due to your handling of him.

Some people simply ignore their babies' crying at night and feel proud of the fact that this successfully "trains" them to sleep through the night, but if you can't do this you must remain firm in your conviction that a crying child needs you and that you are right to go to him.

There are some ways of lessening the burden. Try to have an evening out together from time to time—perhaps book a baby-sitter for a few days ahead to give you something to work toward. If breast-feeding, start expressing milk a few days ahead and storing it in the freezer to make sure you have built up enough supplies for the evening out, so you won't be anxious (page 20). If you have difficulty getting a reliable baby-sitter you might be able to swap evenings with a couple who also have a young baby; they could bring their baby to your house in a carry cot for the evening and you could do the same for them on a later occasion.

If you are breast-feeding, once you get into the habit of expressing milk it can be very helpful in enabling you

"You could try putting books in the corner of his crib."

to get some rest. Let your husband do a couple of nights with expressed milk in a bottle for the baby while you sleep—but make sure you're in a room far enough away not to be able to hear him, or you will be half listening all night. Leave a bottle with someone during the day occasionally, so that you can go out with a friend or even just take the opportunity to do a little quiet shopping on your own. Don't forget the leakage problem if you're out when you would normally be feeding. I couldn't find any breast pads in the house the other evening and went rushing out to the first night of *Starlight Express* with one-way diaper liners stuffed down my bra. They seemed to do the trick, luckily.

Get to know other parents of young babies by going to local play groups, mother and baby groups, playgrounds, etc. It can be very comforting to know just how normal it is for babies to wake at night, and it's always a welcome relief to talk about it.

Don't hesitate to use a pacifier if it helps the family to get a few hours precious sleep (page 55). Ignore people who make you feel guilty by showing their disapproval.

Bring the baby into your bed whenever it feels right to do so; it is a very natural thing to do and far more commonly practiced than many people let on (page 33).

Accept the fact that sleep will be in short bursts rather than the long stretches you are used to. After each time you have fed the baby and settled him, try to relax yourself, so that you can get back to sleep as quickly as possible. Don't lie there straining to catch every sound the baby makes—if he does need you he'll soon let you know, and if he doesn't you're wasting valuable sleep time. On the other hand, if you're having difficulty getting back to sleep don't get too wound up about it—it's not the end of the world and you can survive on a remarkably small amount of sleep. Try to lie there thinking about something pleasant; we are often comfortingly told that these wakeful babies are likely to be very bright children: picture the little darling at the top of his class and imagine how proud you'll be. . . .

Don't worry about anything in the middle of the night—everything really will seem different in the morning. Put off any serious thinking until you are in a better mood; any decision you make at three in the morning will almost certainly have to be rethought out the next day.

Remember you're not the only parent who has spent several months walking around all day like a zombie. You will survive this lack of sleep and even get used to the strange light-headed feeling it gives you.

Do get your partner or a relative or friend to take over the baby for a couple of hours during the day when you get really overtired, so that you can catch up on some sleep. Don't be tempted to use the time to do all those things you've been unable to do with a demanding baby around—go straight to bed and SLEEP! Remember, once you've slept everything will seem much more possible and you'll have twice the energy.

Don't blame your partner or the poor baby in the middle of the night.

Suspend all judgments on anything until the morning. Write down any bad thoughts you have, it's a good way of getting them out of your system. There's no point in two of you being awake, so if you are breast-feeding you do the nights and let your partner take over the baby at some point during the day so that you can catch up.

Make yourself sleep during the day whenever the baby does.

SINGLE PARENTS

I have assumed throughout the book that both parents will be sharing in every aspect of looking after the baby, including the difficult nights. There are of course many mothers and fathers who either through choice or force of circumstances are bringing up babies on their own, or who have a partner unwilling to share the responsibilities and problems that having a family brings.

If you have any relatives who may be willing to help, don't be afraid to ask them. It can be quite flattering to be needed, and often grandparents or uncles or aunts like to show off how well they can handle a baby. Our society makes it very difficult to bring up a child on your own, since our families are frequently so split up and dispersed, unlike the old days of close communities.

Make sure you go to your local clinic regularly, and ask your doctor about any particular problems with sleeping that you may have. You are bound to meet other parents of young children while you are there—try to get chatting to them. It can be enormously helpful to have someone to talk to, and if you become friendly you may be able to help each other with baby-sitting later.

Don't feel you're alone in having terrible nights and some miserable days; it's almost certainly not your fault that the baby doesn't sleep well.

Bring him into your bed if it helps you both to sleep. You may well enjoy each other's company, and at least you don't have a jealous partner to cope with!

USEFUL ADDRESSES

Lewis of London
Branches nationwide
or write to:
215 East 51st Street
New York, NY 10022
(212) 688-3669
For the following baby products:
Natural baby fleeces (lambskins)
"Womb music" teddy bears
Carry cots and baskets
Baby carriers
Three-way adjustable-height drop-sided crib
Swinging cradles
Strolee windup musical swinging
cradle/baby-swing combination
"Bed bag" travel bed
Reclining car seats
Baby walkers
Baby Bjorn baby bouncer

Mothercare
Branches nationwide
or write for catalogue to:
Mothercare by Post
P.O. Box 145
Waterford, Herts, England WD2 5SH
Excellent for baby stretch suits and baby bags.

Mr. and Mrs. Howard Owens
Lullababy, Leominster, England HR6 9BR
Telephone 054-47-630
For the Lullababy vertical rocker and other products.

Toys 'n Things Press
906 North Dale Street
St. Paul, MN 55103
For *Directory of U.S. Toy Lending Libraries* and *The Toy Library How-To Handbook*. Enclose $8.95 plus $1.50 for postage and handling for each brochure.

National Center for Homeopathy
1500 Massachusetts Avenue N.W., Suite 41
Washington, DC 20005
(202) 223-6182

Child Welfare League of America
67 Irving Place
New York, NY 10003
(212) 254-7410

Family Service Association of America
245 West 31st Street
Twelfth floor
New York, NY 10001
(212) 967-2740

National Headquarters
11700 West Lake Park Drive
Park Place
Milwaukee, WI 53224
1-800-967-2740
Referrals for parents of hyperactive children and
counseling on all aspects of family life and problems,
through local agencies.

La Leche League
Chapters nationwide
Or contact:
9616 Minneapolis Avenue
Franklin Park, IL 60131
(312) 455-7730
For information on breast pumps and breast-feeding,
referrals to companies which rent electric breast pumps,
and many other helpful services.

YMCA/YWCA
Branches nationwide
For Water Babies infant and toddler swimming
instruction program

American Herb Association
P.O. Box 353
Rescue, CA 95672
(916) 626-5046

PARENTS • DOCTORS • CHILDCARE SPECIALISTS

Get invaluable information, plus answers to questions, about the toddlers you care for.

by Brooke McKamy Beebe

☐ **BEST BESTS FOR BABIES** • Creative, doctor-approved, and parent-tested advice (more than 100 mothers contributed their suggestions!) on everyday problems of baby's first two years. The text is arranged under broad categories such as "The First Weeks at Home," "Crying," "Games, Toys, and Amusements," and "Health," with one- and two-sentence tips listed therein. A perfect format for busy people like you who want their information in short, easy-to-read nuggets. One tip: hang mirrors or mirrored tiles at baby's eye level in places where she is likely to see them often. Babies *adore* mirrors! $6.95   50453-8

☐ **TIPS FOR TODDLERS** • More time-saving, trouble-saving tips, tailored to the needs of those terrific (but terrible) two- and three-year olds. Again in one- and two-sentence segments, the author provides advice on toilet training, discipline, sleeping, and nursery school. One imaginative idea to allay a child's night fears: keep a lighted fish tank in his or her bedroom. It's good company and a *great* night light! $6.95   58658-5

At your local bookstore or use this handy coupon for ordering:

Dell **DELL READERS SERVICE—DEPT.**
6 REGENT ST., LIVINGSTON, N.J. 07039

Please send me the above title(s). I am enclosing $_____(please add 75¢ per copy to cover postage and handling). Send check or money order—no cash or CODs. Please allow 3-4 weeks for shipment.

Ms./Mrs./Mr._____

Address_____

City/State_____Zip_____